IN THE GLOW OF THE LAVALAMP

*Stories of Bad Sex
and
Other Misfortunes*

Lily Wilson

WANDERING IN THE WORDS PRESS

Copyright © 2017 Lily Wilson.

All rights reserved. No part of this book may be reproduced, stored in a retrieval system or transmitted in any form or by any means without the prior written consent of the publishers, except by a reviewer who may quote brief passages in a review to be printed in a newspaper, magazine, blog, or journal.

To request permission, visit
www.wanderinginthewordspress.com.

PUBLISHED BY WANDERING IN THE WORDS PRESS

ISBN-10: 0-9976355-6-8
ISBN-13: 978-0-9976355-6-0
First Edition

This book is dedicated to the people
who have encouraged me,
my Everybody.

CONTENTS

PART ONE: Bad Sex — 1

Introduction — 2

The Fairy Queen — 5

In Which I Try to Avoid the Inevitable — 16

I Sorry — 27

The Interruption — 33

Can't See the Forest for the Cat's Ass — 40

Stayin' Alive — 48

OK Stupid — 59

The Battle Below the Clouds — 65

Obligated — 75

The Adjunct — 84

PART TWO: Other Misfortunes — 92

The Sample — 93

The Christmas Tree — 100

Big Luck — 105

The Funeral Weekend — 111

Acknowledgements — 124

The world is round and the place which may seem like the end may also be only the beginning.

—Ivy Baker Priest

PART ONE
Bad Sex

INTRODUCTION

What could be more universal than sex? Maybe disappointment? Maybe *bad* sex?

What besides sex is so fraught with hopes, dreams, obsessions, fears, desires, and eagerness? What else has more uncontrollable components and is so dependent on the good will of other people? What has more potential to go in the ditch?

When I first mentioned collecting stories on the topic of bad sex, a surprising number of people said, "Oh, I've got one for you!" I was astounded at how quick people were to share their experiences. Complete strangers emailed me with their stories. Perhaps sex goes badly quite as often as it goes well, but nobody mentions it. Sometimes it goes in the ditch, and rather than see it as part of being human, we see it as failure, shame, or at best, something to be quickly forgotten.

We assume everyone else is having a grand old time between the sheets and we are the only ones with an unsatisfactory experience. So many of us think we are the only ones who ever. The only ones who wanted such and such, who dared to refuse this, agreed to that, or had the gall to request the other thing. We alone have suffered because of faulty assumptions, miscommunication, no communication, or trying too hard. The desire to please can be wonderful and can also backfire horribly. Accidents, interruptions, mismatched longings, health issues, history, ignorance, unrealistic expectations—a million things can derail the experience for one or both. Whether one aspires to enjoy a one-night stand, a glorious fusion of love, or something in between, the possibility of disaster is always present.

Think about it—the act itself is dependent on things ourhumans cannot necessarily control: our bodies and our emotions. And even if one successfully manages those things, the partner may not be managing their own. History can rear its head, dredging up shame, sadness, and resentment. Just getting naked propels one into glaring vulnerability.

Sex is not for the faint of heart. It's for the brave, reckless, or drunk. It drags whatever issues you have out into the often unflattering light.

And to those for whom the words "bad" and "sex" have never before been joined, I submit these offerings as a primer: Yes, that's why she quit taking your calls. It wasn't the flu after all.

I've tried to present each story with the soul of the incident intact, although names, identifying information, and in some cases, chronology of events have been changed. As to the question, *Did this really happen?* The answer is yes, yes indeed it happened—probably way more than once.

Everybody who's had sex more than a time or two has had lousy sex. It's a package deal; your body and mind have the potential to live this glorious experience, and sometimes it will go horribly. The remedies are mainly palliative—laughing about it and realizing you've got lots of company. Welcome to the club.

THE FAIRY QUEEN

Roseanne
Age 25
May 1999

THE FAIRY QUEEN

"Can I see the costume?" I asked.

"Sure." Scott gestured toward the piles of silk flowers and ribbon. "It's here—we'll assemble it as we go."

We were in the guest bedroom of his mother's lavish home, knee deep in mountains of net and fake wisteria he claimed would set up a prize-winning photograph.

"I thought it might be a flowy nightgown Art Nouveau type thing," I said, reddening.

"Oh, please. Darling, no. We're going for a Shakespearean fairy here, not your great Aunt Edna who hasn't left the house in five years."

"I didn't mean like that." My voice cracked. "Not an old lady, but kind of elegant, and...and pretty."

"Hon, you're gonna be way more than pretty." He loaded the glue gun. "You'll be gorgeous, and I'll win the contest. You can crop one of the photos and use it for a head shot."

"I don't need a head shot," I said, feeling like a chubby eighth grader.

"Someday you'll be forty years old and thrilled to have a stunning picture of yourself at twenty-five. You're going to be fabulous. You'll love it. Love. It. I promise. Now relax. Think of it like Halloween, dressing up!"

"OK," I said. "I like Halloween." It was true. Halloween had always been my excuse to try to be girly and beautiful, which otherwise had been frowned upon in the strict religious household where I'd grown up.

"Of course you do," he said. "Now sit here and lean up against the headboard, so I can outline you. This bed is a French antique, and my mother would kill me if she had any idea I was drawing on it. We've got the matching dresser and there's still a label in the drawer. A label—the dealer told us with that in place, the set might be worth $10,000 or more. Not much wicker furniture from that period has survived."

"Maybe we could use something less valuable for the scenery." I sat stiffly while he drew around my torso and head with blue chalk, directly on the white wicker headboard. "Your mother already hates me."

"She doesn't hate you. She thinks of you as somebody from a different culture."

"She called me a tramp."

"Because you have a pick-up truck. Don't take it personally. Since kindergarten, she's been hoping I'll find some Barbie doll who'll convert me. She's just mad you aren't that girl." He rolled his eyes. "She's not here now, so forget it. This is going to be awesome. You'll look so beautiful you're going to be begging for another photo shoot. And I'll be famous—like a *Vogue* cover."

We spent what seemed like hours weaving ribbon and silk flowers in and out of the headboard, using curved crochet hooks and surgical needles. At one point I heard a stem of two-hundred-year-old wicker snap when I pulled too hard. Fortunately, Scott had gone downstairs for glue sticks, so I wedged in a spray of wisteria to cover the hole and smiled innocently when he returned.

"Now it's time for your makeup, and I'm just the one to do it," he said.

"Sure," I said. "I have no idea what it's supposed to look like."

"Like Spenser's 'Faerie Queene!' Like Titania! A gorgeous magical creature of the woodlands."

He plugged in a set of hot rollers and smoothed the primer over my face. His turquoise fishing tackle box had more makeup in it than I'd owned in my entire life.

Every woman should have a gay friend who wants to make her beautiful, although more than once I'd wished he was straight.

The Fairy Queen

The bond we'd forged in grad school was sweet, strong, and better than what I generally had with guys I dated. I told myself it was best this way; it was weird enough to be made up like a sixteenth-century fairy, and would've been weirder still to be on the precious antique bed seething with romance over gorgeous art boy whose mama hates me.

When my hair was in curlers and my face was done, he looked at me with satisfaction. "Take off your clothes. We need to do your torso."

"Do what to my torso?"

He wiggled his eyebrows. "You name it, honey, we're going to do it. C'mon, off, off!"

"No." I crossed my arms over my ribs. "This is too—I can't do that."

"Fine, have it your way." He sighed and walked to the closet, threw something made of orange terrycloth in my direction, and pointed to the bathroom. "Go put this on. And don't mess up your face."

The thing had to be his mother's; it reeked of My Sin or worse. I pulled the elastic band high up over my chest. It was like a strapless, terrycloth bathing suit, but it came down to my knees. My shoulders relaxed, and it all started to feel more possible.

I caught my face in the mirror and almost screamed. I looked like a feral opera singer, ready to play Queen of the Night in Mozart's "Magic Flute" for an audience at a distance of approximately ten thousand feet. It was both thrilling and scary. I looked like I might devour someone's soul, or at least their innocence.

This was exactly why I'd not been allowed to wear makeup as an adolescent. All my life I'd had a want-it-and-fear-it yearning to be beautiful. I heard frequently from my scowling mother that I was "plenty pretty," as if being beautiful would be whorish, shallow, and dangerous, and some unnamed terrible thing would result. I'd felt like a slut before I even knew what a slut was, for wanting to be one notch past plain.

"C'mon! The makeup guy is on the clock," Scott yelled from the other side of the door.

I burst out of the bathroom, emboldened by my exotic, predatory face. "Chill, makeup guy."

"Sit here and lean on the wall." He pointed at a towel on the floor. "Hold your arms out to the side, palms up."

He dusted my arms, collarbones, and neck with a sparkly powder and stepped back to look. "You need more blush."

"Like a hole in my head I do. I already look like some Kabuki player."

"Not on your face. Be still."

He applied a powdery blush to my shoulders, and once again stood back. "That's nice, but I'm thinking maybe a cream base would be better. Hang on."

He dug through the tackle box and found several tubes of goo, which he rubbed into my shoulders and across the bridge of my nose. "We want you to have that sun-kissed look," he said.

With no warning, he tugged the terrycloth wrap down to my waist and began applying the blush across the tops of my breasts.

"Hey!" I clutched at the wrap and stared straight ahead. "You're supposed to ask first."

"I would have, but I was afraid the answer would last till Christmas," he said, continuing to rub the makeup in. "Good grief, we've been skinny dipping."

He peered at my chest as if it were an eye chart. "I'm going to highlight the sides of them, so they'll be all glowy."

"Just get it done. I'm cold."

"Well, you can't put that thing back on. It'll rub your makeup off. I'll get you a sheet."

Finally, draped in a sheet, the orange wrap drooping around my waist, my hair sprayed into curls that could withstand a week in a wind tunnel, I was ready. He had me sit in front of the headboard, where the chalk outline of me looked like a crime scene.

"Ribbon," he said. "We need more ribbon—and scarves."

"Whatever." I coughed from the hair spray. "I need a gas mask and a drink."

"That's the spirit. Be right back."

Moments later he returned with two glasses of chardonnay and set one on either side of me.

"Where's yours?"

"The photographer doesn't drink; those are for you."

"Excellent." I took a good long sip.

He wrapped ivory and gold satin ribbons around my feet and twined them up my calves like Roman sandals. A long filmy scarf snaked around my hips, tied in a giant complex knot in front.

I finished the first glass of wine with a chipper little gulp. "My loins are girded now," I said.

"Yep." He grabbed the scissors, chopped the orange wrap in two, and pulled it from my waist.

"Your mom won't mind a bit, I'm sure." I flashed my eyebrows at him.

"She'll never miss it." He stuffed it halfway into a duffle bag. "I didn't want to ruin the Gordian knot in the scarf—it's perfect."

A gentle wine buzz rippled through my belly and chest.

"I've got a surprise for you, Sweet Pea," he said.

"OK!" I was becoming more amiable by the minute. "What is it?"

"Sweet peas. Real live sweet peas for Sweet Pea." He brought out a stem from behind his back. "You have no idea what I went through to get these."

They were exquisite. A deep, fuchsia-tinged purple, cascading like a vine from a stoppered test-tube gizmo with a little water in it. I reached for them.

"Ah ah ah, not yet!" he said. "Wait till we get everything set up. Then you can hold them for the shoot."

"What else is there to get ready?"

He handed me the second glass of wine. "You just leave that to me, my pretty."

"OK," I said, sipping.

"Let's have some music." He slipped a cassette into the boom box. "You'll love this. It's a bona fide mix tape—remember those? Slow jazz."

A champagne river of piano music swirled around me. I beamed, all tingly and fortunate.

Thirty minutes later, my arms and hair, yes, my actual hair, were attached to the wicker headboard with an intricate ribbon weaving. He placed cushions under my elbows; otherwise I'd never have been able to hold my arms up like that for long. I marveled at his patience; this guy who couldn't tolerate the five minutes it took for a Windows update, spent a half hour weaving braids with skinny silk ribbons into my hair and threading the curls into the headboard. When he held up a giant mirror, I had to admit the effect was stunning. I was stunning. I looked like I was underwater, with the currents waving my hair into mermaid-esque curves. The opera makeup now looked radiant, not frightening. Scott knew what he was doing.

He took some practice shots, frowned, and set the camera down. He dusted the sparkly powder on my legs and put quite a lot on my feet, even. My inner arms got a similar tickly dosing.

I realized for the first time ever that my plump arms were nice. Really nice. "My curvy, pouty biceps are blushing," I said, laughing.

"Girl, they are." He smiled and nipped at one, his lips covering his teeth. "Your whole body is blushing like a bowl of peach ice cream. Scrumptious."

I nudged him with one of my glittery feet. "Some might say that this is a set up for seduction," I said. I slowly closed my eyes, and then opened them.

"Some might." He crawled slowly toward me, his face stopping inches away, his green eyes staring into mine. "You are magnificent."

I felt gorgeous, relaxed into it, and wondered why beauty had ever seemed bad. Beauty was a glorious thing. I sighed and thought about how much of life my mother had missed out on with her fear of loveliness. I was meant to be here, right now, in this moment, in this place, exuding joy and splendor like rays of sun.

"If my arms weren't attached to this headboard, I'd kiss you now," I said. Where the hell had that come from? I wanted him. No two ways about it. I wanted him and I was now gorgeous and we both knew it. There would never be a better time.

"Yeah?" he said.

"Yeah. Come here."

He brushed his cheek against my face, like a cat. "The one thing that might heighten your glory would be a little aroused glow."

"It's possible I already have that particular glow," I said.

"Yeah?" he softly pressed his mouth on mine.

The kiss was everything—soft, tender, hinting at a raw, barely restrained riptide of passion—on my side anyway.

"I've wanted to do this for a long time."

I nibbled at his lower lip. "But I thought…I thought you liked men." My guts fizzed with vertigo and desire.

"I do. I like men. I like women. I like humans. I'm very particular that way."

My head spun, and my body was lighting up with *Oh hallelujah, yes!*

"You're pretty damn irresistible." He peeled off his shirt. "I want to be sure we have the same idea about this, though."

"This what?"

"Sexual healing." He ran the back of his hand over the soft part of my inner arm. "Should I get a condom?"

"Get one, Marvin," I said. "Yes, yes, yes, please."

He happened to have a condom in the fishing tackle box.

Quick as lightning, the question zipped through my brain, *Did I set this up?* Then, *Did he?*

Before he tore the condom open, he flipped the mix tape, and Diana Krall was on the other side, pouring out her sultry version of "I've Got You Under My Skin." I felt a year's worth of endorphins coursing in my blood, and I smiled and thanked God that Diana Krall existed and had recorded that song.

And the wine, along with the rest of me said, *Who cares who set it up? It's the most shimmering thing ever!*

In a short time, Scott was wearing as much of the sparkly powder as I was. I couldn't move around much, as my hands, hair, and arms were firmly anchored to the headboard like Gulliver, tied down by the Lilliputians. My glistening legs and feet remained untethered though, and my inhibitions lay in shreds, like the orange terry wrap.

Soon my ribbon-sandaled feet were resting on his shoulders, shedding iridescent bits down onto his chest, and nothing, nothing had ever felt more right. "Aha ahaaaa," I said.

"I've got yooooooou under my skin," he sang along.

Being beautiful was better than I'd ever imagined.

I felt something tickling on the side of my hip. I couldn't move my head to see, but something was there, brushing against the tip top of my thigh on the side.

"On the left." I gasped. "Get it, get it, please, on the left!"

Misunderstanding, he leaned to the left and focused his attentions there, and I felt something brush against me with each thrust. Whatever it was felt big, and I imagined a set of giant hairy insect legs hanging off him, swinging forward and repeatedly grasping at me.

"Scott! It's a big spider on the—" With a shriek I shoved his shoulders hard with my silvery feet. It was an involuntary movement, and he went flying back, cock pointing straight up, his back arched, sweet peas trailing him like a flouncy magenta horse's tail. His head hit the floor with a loud *thunk*.

"Scott? You OK?" I struggled to sit up, unable to move my head or arms more than half an inch.

"Scott! Can you hear me?" No answer and no answer and no answer came back.

Diana Krall sang on.

"Uh," said Scott.

I was pinned down like a butterfly on a naturalist's board. I waved my feet in the air, trying to gain traction.

"Sco-ottt, Scott!" I tugged my head, trying to free it. Such a thorough job he'd done weaving me into the headboard with so many strands of hair and so many ribbons—I gained no ground.

"Owwwr," he said, sounding more like a bear than a human.

I thrashed with my feet, and got a rocking motion going. Maybe I could lift the headboard off of the frame. With a massive heave, I pulled up and out. Nothing. I tried again and heard cracking. So what if I damaged the fasteners.

"Ow," he said. "Ouch. Hit my head."

"Do you want an ice pack? I'll take you for stitches." I gave a karate-type shriek, made a bold surge, and the wicker behind me went *snap, creak, slither* as I pulled free.

Half the headboard came with me.

Like Medusa with her snaky hair and arms wired to the side of a giant Easter basket, I lurched forward and scrambled to my feet. Arms frozen, one above, and one beside my head, I hobbled over to him.

A door slammed downstairs and a woman's voice called, "Yoo-hoo! Scott, honey? You up here?"

His mother.

Diana Krall had gotten horribly, obscenely, loud, singing "Do it Again." For an instant I considered throwing the boom box through the glass window, as if that would fix everything, if only she'd shut up.

Footsteps knocked along on the hardwood floor, and his mom started up the stairs, sounding like she had on wooden shoes.

"Scott," I bent over him, the wicker backdrop to my head casting a shadow, "I'll cover you." I lunged at the orange terry wrap, threw it toward him, and scanned the room for a hiding place.

I was trying to wedge myself and my beribboned wicker regalia into the closet when she entered the room. She stepped over the turquoise tackle box and the hot rollers, stood, hands on hips, and stared without moving a muscle in her face. Her eyes jumped wildly, taking everything in.

Buck naked beyond a pound of makeup and ribbons, head and arms attached to half her priceless headboard, I turned to face her. I stepped out toward Scott, who—sprawled naked, the orange wrap on his shoulder catching a little blood from where he'd hit his head—had a spray of sweet peas blooming from his butt. I might as well have said, yes, I am in fact, Kali the Destroyer. Instead I said,

"Those sweet peas, I thought they were a spider on me."

IN WHICH I TRY TO AVOID THE INEVITABLE

by Jonathan Hart Price

Kyle
Age 18
1997

IN WHICH I TRY TO AVOID THE INEVITABLE

By Jonathan Hart Price

"It's dark back here."

"I know. We don't want anyone to see what we're doing, do we?"

"I guess not. It seems a little creepy, though."

"Don't worry, nobody can see us back here. We've got the whole parking lot to ourselves. Here, I'll turn the stereo on…hey…look at me, baby."

"I'm sorry, it's just…it's just that I'm not sure if this is how I pictured it or not."

"It doesn't matter how you pictured it. It's going to be special because we make it special, because we love each other. I'm wearing that dress you like."

"I do love you. You look nice. What record is this—is this Tool?"

In Which I Try to Avoid the Inevitable

"Yeah, it's *Undertow*. You have this record, too, I know you like it."

"I do, and I do like it, but…you don't have anything else?"

"No, this is the only CD I keep in my mom's car. Remember? It's the CD that was on when we first kissed."

"What song is this? Is this 'Prison Sex'?"

"Um, yeah I think it is."

"You don't think that's weird? We should put on some Marvin Gaye or something or Barry White or Al Green or something like that. Not 'Prison Sex.'"

"I told you, this is the only CD I keep in my mom's car. Come on, let's just get in the back seat and stop worrying about it."

"I'm not worried about it. I'm just saying that maybe this isn't the best choice of song for what we're about to do. Do you hear what he's saying? What is he saying?"

"It's a beautiful song. You just have to listen to it. Here, I'll turn it up a little. See? He's talking about his precious lamb, saying that for one sweet moment he feels whole. That's beautiful, don't you think? That's what I want it to be like for us. One sweet moment, where we both come together—two precious lambs who make each other whole. There's nothing wrong with this song—it's perfect."

"It's not about two lambs becoming whole in one precious moment or whatever, it's a song about child abuse. Maynard's singing about how his stepfather molested him or beat him up or something."

"Well, that's not what I get out of it. It's a beautiful song, and that's what it means to me. That's what it means to me when I think about us."

"Have you ever heard this song before?"

"Are you getting smart? Of course I have, about a thousand times. Every time I hear it I think about us."

"Really? I mean, I understand people get different things out of music, but come on—you mean to tell me you heard him singing about being tied up and getting blood on his hands, and you thought of us living together in perfect harmony?"

"Stop being a jerk. I'm not interested in the literal meaning of the song. I'm just interested in you, baby. This is a pointless discussion. It doesn't matter anyway. The song will be over in a little bit."

"You know, you did the same thing with 'Brick.'"

"With what?"

"You know, the Ben Folds song? 'She's a brick and I'm drowning' and all that? That song came on the radio the first time we ever came over here, like three months ago, and you told me that you wanted that to be our song, that you thought it was beautiful how he described being powerless against the girl he

In Which I Try to Avoid the Inevitable

was with, that they fell for each other completely, and you wanted that to be us."

"I love that song."

"And I told you that it's not about falling in love; it's about his girlfriend getting an abortion."

"What about when he tells his family about the two of them?"

"What, in 'Brick'? He's not telling his family about some hidden romance; he's telling his family about how he knocked up his girlfriend and she had to get rid of it, that he was tired of keeping it a secret. Is that how you think about us? That being together is like hiding a terrible secret? Because that's what it sounded like when you told our friends that 'Brick' was our song. That's why they all rolled their eyes."

"What the hell is that supposed to mean? You're being irrational, and I don't care what Ben Folds was singing about. I think of us every time I hear that song, and I never think about somebody getting an abortion. Besides, how do you know what it means? We were listening to the same song. Maybe you're the one who heard it wrong."

"It doesn't matter."

"No, it doesn't. And besides, we agreed that 'Brick' didn't have to be our song. It can be something else, and 'Prison Sex' just happened to come on just now, so that doesn't have to be our song, either. What's wrong with you—don't you love me?"

"I do love you."

"Then it shouldn't matter what song is playing. It's just you and me here right now, together, and we're about to do something that we'll remember for the rest of our lives. We won't remember what song was playing. We'll just remember how we felt when we gave in to everything that makes us human. I love you."

"No, I'll remember it. I'll remember that we had this conversation, too."

"I don't get it. Why are you being so confrontational, don't you want to be here? What sixteen-year-old guy wouldn't want to be here with his beautiful girlfriend, who wants nothing more than to get naked with him and let him do anything he wants to her. Are you out of your mind?"

"You are beautiful."

"Do you love me?"

"Of course."

"Then what's the problem? Just get in the back seat."

"I just don't think 'Prison Sex' is appropriate—that's all I'm trying to say. It's disturbing, and it's making me uncomfortable."

"This is so frustrating. You haven't been that picky about what was on the stereo when we were out here doing all that other stuff.

In Which I Try to Avoid the Inevitable

This isn't the first time we've been to this parking lot, you know."

"Yeah, I know. Like I said, there was the time we came here and listened to 'Brick.'"

"That was the first time we parked here. We've done plenty more since then, and you've never said anything about what CD was playing. And you didn't feel uncomfortable, that's for sure. I think you felt exactly the opposite."

"I know, but this time it's more…serious, so much more serious, and those other times, that other stuff, most of that was nothing I couldn't have done on my own."

"Nobody's that flexible."

"I said most of that other stuff. You know what I mean."

"Uh-huh."

"This just isn't how I pictured it. Is this how you pictured it? Is this how you wanted it to happen—in the back seat of your mother's car in a dark parking lot, listening to Tool?"

"No. No, this is absolutely not how I pictured it. I pictured it happening two weeks ago when we went to Aaron Lindroth's house after prom. We had the whole basement to ourselves, and you didn't want to do anything because you thought somebody might come downstairs or they'd hear us or we'd make a mess or something like that. That's how I pictured it, but it didn't work out like that— because you were too scared, that's why. That was how I wanted it, and we won't ever have another chance like that. And we might not have another chance like this one, either. What requirements am I not fulfilling here?"

"I don't know."

"We just have to make the best of it, and that's what I'm trying to do."

"I know you are, and I appreciate that. I do love you, and I want this for us."

"Great, me too. So let's get in the back."

"Why don't we just wait a little bit? Why don't we plan it out, like get a hotel room out of town or something—a nice room with champagne and all that, with roses on the nightstand. Somewhere we can be gentle with one another, where we won't feel so rushed."

"I don't feel rushed—and we do have a plan. You promised me the morning after prom that we could set a date for this, and today's the day. You promised me that no matter what, we would make it happen. You didn't say anything about hotel rooms or roses. You just told me that you loved me and that you'd make it up to me on this very night, and here we are. I've been driving all over town with nothing on underneath this dress and I'm starting to get a little impatient."

"I didn't think it through. We could plan to go away and really do something special."

"It doesn't matter where we are—it's going to be special."

In Which I Try to Avoid the Inevitable

"We can plan the music out better, too, so we can have more than one CD with us. Then we won't have to listen to Maynard singing about there being a release in sodomy."

"Does he say that?"

"Yes, he does...listen...there it is."

"I thought he was saying 'release inside of me,' like he was feeling relieved."

"No, he is most definitely talking about forcible sodomy, which I think is both conceptually and quite literally exactly what we're trying to avoid here."

"I'm not trying to avoid anything. You're the one who's being slippery about it."

"Slippery?"

"Slippery. You're the one trying to weasel his way out of this when you know it's exactly what I want. What we want. You got what you wanted all those other times we've been out here, and now it's my turn. This is what I want. I want you to give it to me, and I could care less what CD is playing. Get over yourself, take your pants off, and get in the back seat so we can forget about the meaning of everything and have sex like two normal human beings."

"Now you're the one who's being confrontational."

"Give me a break."

"This is too important to me. You don't think I'll remember this song for the rest of my life? You don't think I'll remember this moment every time I hear this song come on, long after this night has passed, long after you and I have gone to different colleges, moved away, or found a reason to hate each other?"

"Don't you dare say that."

"This song is going to be a part of me forever. It will forever be attached to the first time you and I were together—the first time you and I were together with anyone. And if I can't have the hotel room and the flowers and the luxury of being in a comfortable place, then at the very least we can listen to a song that more aptly defines exactly what we mean to each other, because this memory is going to be permanent—just like when you told me you loved me for the first time, and we were listening to 'Breathe' by Pink Floyd."

"I remember that, of course I do, and I'll remember that for the rest of my life. I get it. And I remember that song, too. I remember digging through my dad's record collection to find something we both liked, figuring out how the turntable worked, feeling your breath against my cheek as we kissed, and how special and spent we felt after it was all over. I remember all of that."

"Of course you do. It was only a week ago."

"Don't be facetious. I remember all of that because it was so pure, so wholesome, and more than anything, I remember it because it was you. Not because of the song. I

In Which I Try to Avoid the Inevitable

don't remember some random hookup with a faceless person while I listened to Roger Waters play the bass line from 'Money.'"

"I love that bass line."

"It's your face in that memory—yours and mine together. That's what's important. And yes, I think of that night every time I hear that song, but it could've been any song, it really could have. You're what makes that memory beautiful, and whatever song was playing at the time would have been made beautiful, too, because of you and me, and how we feel about each other."

"I know. I understand, but 'Prison Sex' is too distracting and it's making me feel weird. Listen to him—talking about the shadow behind him shrouding every step he takes. Does that sound like us to you?"

"Is the song still on? Are we still talking about this?"

"Yeah, it's still on. Listen."

"It's not the same song. It's the next one. This is 'Sober,' the one after 'Prison Sex,' so that proves it doesn't matter. You didn't even notice that the song had changed."

"This one's even worse."

"Are you done being a jerk now? I feel like we've been out here for like an hour. We could have been done by now, cuddling in the back seat, a huge moment in our lives behind us with nothing but each other as far as either of us can see."

"Do you think that's what it's going to be like?"

"I know that's what it's going to be like."

"I don't think it's going to be like that at all, with this kind of music on."

"Fine. I'll just turn it off...there. Problem solved, right? Right? Are you listening to me? Look over here, baby."

"Sorry. Can we turn the radio on or something?"

"The seek button's broken, and all the programmed stations are talk radio."

"Your mother listens to talk radio?"

"Yeah—flat tax, idiot liberals, gun rights, the whole mess. You wanna lose your virginity to Rush Limbaugh? I sure as hell don't."

"Just turn the radio on and see if it works. Maybe we'll get a music station or we can find public radio or something."

"Fine...there...oh, Jesus."

"What song is this? Is this 'Brick'?"

"I don't believe this."

"Look, I cannot do this in silence. It's too dark and it's too creepy back here by ourselves. I need something on in the background, but it sure as hell can't be this. It's starting to get late anyway."

"What are you trying to say? We can let this song play out and then we'll get down to business. Come on, let's climb over the seats into the back, and by the time we get settled

In Which I Try to Avoid the Inevitable

the song will be over. Come on, it's now or never."

"We've already been over this. If we start doing what we're doing while this song is on, it's just going to make things worse."

"You're not making any sense."

"And what if the next song that comes on isn't right, either? Are we going to stop? When that moment comes, when we're really getting into it—you've got your skirt up around your hips, my pants around my ankles—what if something even worse comes on? Think about it...what if we're halfway there when 'Cat's in the Cradle' starts playing?"

"Are you out of your mind?"

"At least with a CD, we have control. We know ahead of time if all the songs are going to be right for us. The radio might be better than Tool, but it's too unpredictable, and I'm not at all comfortable with that."

"Then what do you want to do?"

"Let's just go back to your house, and we can figure this out later. It's already been a rough night, and I'm sorry—I'm sorry I brought all this up. Let's just forget about it and start fresh tomorrow. There will be plenty of other times. I don't think we should have sex in your mom's car anyway, but that's another issue."

"Let me ask you something."

"Anything, baby. I love you."

"Are you gay?"

"What?"

"You know my friend Sherri? She told me she thought you were gay. You dress well, you keep your sideburns neat, you smell good, your favorite class is art history—and you told me yourself that your favorite part of Thanksgiving is making pâté with your mother and five aunts. So when I told her all of that—all those reasons why I love you—and she asked why we'd been together for three months and hadn't had sex yet, her only conclusion was that you must be gay."

"That's ridiculous. Sherri's ridiculous."

"What kind of man wouldn't want to do this right here, right now, no matter what? Your fit, beautiful girlfriend is sitting across from you in a sundress with nothing on underneath—and yes, I'm freezing now, by the way—begging you to have sex with her, and you're making excuses. So what am I supposed to think? This doesn't seem like the kind of situation a straight man would turn down. There's nothing about this that seems weird or uncomfortable to me. This is amazing. This is what fantasies are made of—what they make porn films about. Two young lovers who'll go to any length to get what they want, which is each other. That doesn't seem hot to you?"

"I'm not gay."

In Which I Try to Avoid the Inevitable

"Well then, I tell you what I'm going to do. I'm going to put the Tool CD back in the stereo. Then I'm going to turn the stereo back on and play it from the top, just to show you it doesn't matter, and I promise you, you won't even notice. Then, I'm going to lay down in the back seat and wait for you."

"I think I'm going to be sick."

"Shut up and take your pants off."

"Fine."

"Love you."

"Love you too."

I SORRY

Belinda
Age: 30
Date: 1987

I SORRY

My boyfriend had begun bragging to me about the women he flirted with, almost like a child boasting of his accomplishments. He ogled other women when we were out together. I felt the floor creaking and sagging under my feet, but no one thing was big and ugly enough to make me leave.

I know it's hard to imagine how such a man might hold a lot of appeal, and it's harder still considering he'd begun to speak baby talk at odd moments. Standing in the elevator, he'd gaze at me, touch my arm, and say in his baby-esque voice, "I love" or even "I love?"

Simply, "I love." He couldn't incorporate a direct object. He couldn't acknowledge there was a significant, or even an insignificant other.

Once, when he poisoned a sweet moment with his, "I love?" like a toddler's question, it occurred to me he might be stuck in some infantile stage like a baby who hasn't yet learned to differentiate his mother from himself. The whole world to a baby is one big *me*. His discomfort, his desire to be held, his need to clamp his lamprey-like mouth and tiny hands upon a nurturing breast—the whole world is *him*. Any indication of separateness, such as the breast or his blankie being withdrawn before he pushes it away, brings outrage. And when the desired item is returned, he's one big happy "I love."

So alarmed was I by this idea that my boyfriend might be firmly lodged in a pre-sippy-cup developmental stage, that I quickly pushed it aside. In fact, I carried it to the backyard and buried it deep.

Thus, we limped along as a couple, his most intimate murmurings consisting of "I love" and occasionally, "I sorry." Yeah, "I sorry," spoken exactly like that. Not only could he not say the word "you," he also seemed unable to form the contraction, "I'm." He usually served up the "I sorry" in reference to things over which he had no control—for example, in response to the observation that the wind was blowing.

I'll call him Babyman. He had some endearing qualities. We had similar tastes in music and politics, and a bit of a spark between us. He was a great cook, and his apartment was spotless. In fact, cleanliness was an obsession with him. He scrubbed scuff marks off the baseboards with an old toothbrush. I didn't care about the baseboards, but it was lovely to sleep over where the bathroom was always clean. And he was bright—well, book smart anyhow. At some point, he'd been lots of fun.

The forays into baby talk had thrown a bit of a chill onto our relationship. The more infantile he seemed, and the less able to relate as an adult, the less I wanted him as an intimate partner. I told myself that everybody isn't verbal; every relationship requires compromises, and maybe we could connect by having fun. We cooked together, we listened to music. I tried to recover some connection with him, feeling certain it had been there and I could get it back, all the while doing everything I could to dodge intimacy. I stayed over less, and when I did, came to bed after he had fallen asleep. I'd wake up early and run to the bathroom to dress. The thought of his hands on me, the baby voice chirping, "I love?" got me up and out more reliably than any alarm clock.

I coasted on the fumes of what I thought had once been good, and distrusted my own perspective on both the past and the present. Unable to make a decision to leave, I stayed.

One Friday night we found our way back to good—making pizza and drinking beer. We spooned on the couch, watching a stupid movie, laughing, and working on more beers.

In the Glow of the Lavalamp

He was funny and sweet. We smooched during the commercials. The baby voice was gone. His brown plaid couch scratched the side of my face, and I found it endearing. The yum factor returned, like blood pulsing warmth into a frostbitten limb. I relaxed into being crazy about him again.

We made our way to the bedroom, engaging in a competition to see who could fling their garments the farthest. His wadded up sock, thrown like a baseball, knocked over a vase of dried flowers. He laughed and let it be.

We nipped and teased each other and felt the heat of skin on skin. The glow of his face pressing into my neck was gold, and his beard in the light of the lava lamp reminded me of a wolf. I was hungry for it all. The beer fullness kept us at a leisurely pace, and we were having the most glorious time giggling, flushed with joy. Then he nuzzled up to my ear and whined, "Honey, sometimes I just wish you had a dick."

I heard the needle-scratching-a-record sound and froze. He wanted a guy? Was that the problem? Or he wanted me to get some type of device? Could I do that? Keeping my head very still, I slid a look at him from the corner of my eye.

"It would be so much easier if I could just do to you what I do to myself, instead of having to think about what you like."

Indeed.

A taste for a kink or a toy was one thing. That, I could live with, possibly. Maybe. But he wished he didn't have to acknowledge I was female because it was more trouble than pleasuring himself? I really *was* in bed with a giant baby. This was horrible in a most freeing way. In my mind I saw a door swing open, and my path, clear of any attraction to him, lit up with neon. I knew in that instant I would never be here again in his arms. No amount of beer or fun was ever going to make this OK.

In the same instant, I decided I'd rather go through the motions than confront him, have the talk, and deal with his naked anger. So I reanimated my face and body, and put my emotions firmly aside, with a silent apology.

Just for now. I'll be back for y'all later, and I promise, from now on I'm gonna to listen to everything you say.

On we went. My response to his confession was, "Mmph." I kissed him more, smushed my face into his chest, and tried to rev up the machinery of this the final act.

It went surprisingly well, considering. We were proceeding along splendidly, or he was, and I was doing enough to get by. Then a twinge of discomfort flitted through my gut. And again. Before long I had an undeniable stomach ache.

"Um," I said, trying to roll his weight off me. "Let's try that other position."

He was agreeable, and we shifted accordingly. He seemed pleased with the new arrangement and appeared to be enjoying himself mightily, despite my lack of a male member.

My stomach ache was building steadily to nausea, and soon my entire focus was on trying not to vomit.

Too much food and alcohol, too much motion, and no doubt my feelings about the recently announced penis deficit, overcame me. The beer and pizza came crowding into my mouth, overflowed, and kept coming. I tried to lean forward and send it down the wall behind the bed to the spotless baseboard, but I couldn't reach.

The vomit cascaded onto his shoulder and then split into two streams, fairly evenly distributed, moving down his back and chest where tiny hillocks of goat cheese and green pepper stuck in his manly hairiness.

Anybody who has ever vomited on a shag carpet will have some idea of the difficulties encountered when one pukes onto a hairy partner. He was a bit of a mess.

Babyman was nearing a pinnacle of enjoyment; eyes tightly shut, head thrown back, throat making howling sounds—oblivious. I wiped my mouth on my arm and watched him.

Finally, he reached his destination, slowed, and became still.

"Um," I said. "I got sick." I went to get a towel, happy to leave the area.

He slumped. "Oh man."

While he showered, I changed the bed, rinsed out the sheets, and scrubbed the sink with Ajax, thinking, *I'm not coming back.*

I told him I was sick and had to go home.

He walked me to the door, and avoiding my mouth, kissed my face somewhere up near my ear.

"I love," he said.

I answered with the only words that came to me. "I sorry."

THE INTERRUPTION

*Vivian
Age 26
August 1980*

THE INTERRUPTION

I was raised on disapproval. My parents weren't bad people, just products of an age when praising a child was considered a bad idea. Whether it was penmanship, posture, or attitude—everything was bad, wrong, or in desperate need of improvement. This behavior management strategy worked so well that by age six they could control me with a wrinkled brow or a frown. As a teenager, I was able to anticipate disfavor and plan ahead to sidestep it. Thus, I arrived at adulthood with powerful people-pleasing and avoidance skills, little decision-making ability, and absolutely no conscious awareness of any of this.

One Friday afternoon, my boyfriend Roger and I finished our tennis game and went to my place for beers. Before long we had tossed our clothes and were having loud, thumping, knocking, fun—the kind that evokes jealousy and offends the neighbors.

In the Glow of the Lavalamp

We were lost in this when someone rapped sharply on the door. We froze.

"I'm not answering that," I whispered.

This was our last-chance sex before my mom showed up for a weekend visit. She would arrive at 7 p.m., and before then we had three hours for sex, showers, and dinner. But answering the door to a Jehovah's Witness or some kid selling magazines? No time for that.

The knocking got louder, and a voice wailed, "Vivian! Viviaaannnnn!"

It was my mother. Three hours early.

We were trapped.

The double-edge blade of fear and shame sliced through me. Then fury. Was I not twenty-five years old? Was I not allowed to have a life that included doing normal things-- like having sex with my boyfriend?

She would have strongly disapproved. On a scale of 1 to 10, with 1 being *Enjoy!* and 10 being *How dare you? That's filthy and reprehensible!* her response would have registered at about 357.

She beat on the door a long time. We crawled around on the floor collecting our clothes. Since the curtains were open, we couldn't risk being seen. A peek out the window confirmed that she was in her car, keeping vigil.

A breezeway and stairs ran down the middle of the building. My apartment was on the second floor in front, all windows facing the parking lot and my mom.

Neither Roger nor I had nerves that could withstand waiting her out, so we made a plan, a plan that involved lying and possible injury or death. All of those seemed better than explaining what she'd just interrupted.

We twisted a sheet into a rope. On one end, I tied a knot and hooked a rock climber's carabiner through it. I'd gone rappelling once, and thought this, clipped through a belt loop, was a good safety feature.

Roger would go out first and greet Mom. He'd chat with her and get her to turn away from the building. I would scurry to the back of the breezeway and hide. He would tell her that he'd dropped me off at my sewing club and returned to the apartment to shower off the tennis sweat. Then he'd let her into the apartment to wait for my return.

Once Mom was in the apartment, I'd lower myself to the ground on the sheet, run out to the street, and Roger would drive by to pick me up. What could possibly go wrong?

So he sauntered out the door, and watching him, I saw a mini-pad, creased in half, stuck to the back of his shorts. *No. Nonono.* I'm the one with the mini-pad, and how the hell… I couldn't speak so I hissed at him.

Scowling, he put a finger to his lips. I gestured frantically at the leg of my shorts. He raised both hands as if to say, "What?" shrugged, and moved on, mini-pad in place.

He went down the stairs whistling.

I made it to the back of the breezeway, where I considered jumping to my death, but instead hid behind a storage unit, eyes closed, teeth clenched, while Mom and Roger came up the stairs chatting, went into the apartment, and shut the door.

I tied the sheet to the railing, clipped the carabiner to my belt loops, and climbed over—toes on the cement ledge. The grass and sidewalk looked very far below, but where else could I go? I jumped, letting out enough of the sheet so I wouldn't swing back in and hit the cement floor.

I'd overestimated several things: the strength of my belt loops, the distance to the brick wall, and the length of my makeshift rope. The sheet jerked out of my hands, ripping off both belt loops. I grabbed at the cloth as it untwisted and smacked me into the bricks, knees first. One final twist turned me facing out away from the building.

I slid down clutching the sheet, still far from the ground. Above me, the iron rail had pulled out of the wall and was bending a bit.

At this point a voice in my head said, *If you're adult enough to have sex, you're too adult to be doing stupid things to hide it.*

OK, I thought, *but right now I'm in mid-stupidity.*

The Interruption

My arms stretched over my head, and between the pull of gravity and the torque of the sheet, I worried that my shoulders might come out of the sockets. The sheet continued to untwist. I let go and landed hard on the sidewalk. I ran out to the street, knees bleeding.

Before long, Roger picked me up. The plan had worked. We got out of the apartment without being seen together.

"Well, did she believe you?" I asked.

"Absolutely!" he said.

"Good. Phew."

"Just one thing though." He grinned. "I told her that after tennis, I dropped you at your sewing club and came back for a shower."

"Yeah, that was the plan," I said.

"Right away, she went in the bathroom and threw back the shower curtain. The tub was dry."

My blood ran cold. "What'd you say?"

"Nothing. Just smiled."

"We should have run the shower. I didn't think she'd check."

He laughed. "She can't prove anything."

My guts squeezed. Already she had found a hole in our scheme.

We returned to the apartment, me ready to face a firing squad, and Roger near-euphoric, loving the charade. I walked behind him. The mini-pad was gone. I didn't ask.

I hugged my mother. "Hey, you're early! I hope this guy was good to you."

"What happened to your knees?" she asked.

Her face resembled that of a boarding school headmistress who has just learned that her charges are running a prostitution ring from their dorm.

"I fell, playing tennis, before my sewing club. Did Roger tell you?"

"He mentioned that," she said. "I don't see any sewing."

"I helped with a quilt."

Roger smirked as if I'd claimed I helped Betsy Ross create the flag of our nation.

My mother stared.

We sent Roger to pick up a pizza, and I hoped to God he'd think to remove the sheet waving like a giant white flag of surrender from the bent railing in the back of the breezeway.

After he left, my mom said, "Roger said he'd been taking a shower, but the tub was completely dry."

"Really?" I said. "Just like a kid who pretends to take a bath."

She raised an eyebrow. "I got the impression he was hiding something."

"Well I'd hide it, too, if I was only pretending to bathe."

We set the table in silence, moving around silverware and cups as if they were chess pieces.

"I think Roger was wearing a sanitary pad," my mother said.

I was so angry—angry at how much power she still had over me, at the unfairness of her showing up three hours early without so much as a phone call, and at the infernal persistence of the adhesive on mini-pads. I snapped.

"What?" I yelled. "That's gross! You were staring at his groin."

"I wasn't," she said. "He had—"

"Why don't we let his health concerns be *his* private business."

"He has health concerns?" she asked.

"I wouldn't dream of asking such a personal question," I said, giving her a stern face.

Roger returned, the beaming pizza-bearer, and while we ate, I yammered on about jobs, weather, anything. The two of them said little.

I brought up a radio program I'd heard about how a person's best quality often has a flip slide that makes it their worst fault, too. I explained it all and then explained it again using other words, and kept on like a drunk.

"I'm trying to think if that's true," I said. "If my best quality is being conscientious and responsible, I guess the negative side would be perfectionism?"

"Responsible?" my mother asked. "Really?" She took a sip of water and exhaled loudly.

"What do you think, Mom? What would you say yours is?"

She put her gaze on Roger, like a needle. "Deception," she said.

Roger and I froze as if we were afflicted with some kind of paralysis, and my mom continued to study him and smiled a brittle smile. It came to me that if the Jehovah's Witnesses were to knock on the door now, I would invite them in. But nobody knocked.

The only sound was my mother's water glass being set back down on the table, a soft *clonk*. We looked at each other kind of beady-eyed and wooden.

I turned to her and something strange and new rose up in me. "Don't be too hard on yourself," I said. "Sometimes in the moment, lying feels like the best way to go, even if it's not. Sometimes it feels almost like survival. I get it."

CAN'T SEE THE FOREST FOR THE
CAT'S ASS

Helen
Age 38
November 2010

CAN'T SEE THE FOREST FOR THE CAT'S ASS

Denial is not a river in Egypt, but it may be a river in your hometown. This is the story of a year-long cruise on DeNial. How in the world could somebody stay on the boat for so long when they could leave at any time? Two things: 1. Not acknowledging you're on the boat; and 2. Pretzeling—a technique in which you twist and bend your perspective to fit the situation, no matter how bizarre. You dismiss anything that seems wrong and attribute it to your own failure to adapt or accept others.

So. A cruise, y'all! Pack your Dramamine and come aboard!

The first time I visited my boyfriend's home—let's call him Dave—we watched a movie. His cat, Coco, wandered among our feet and climbed on us. Dave kept pressing her tail down with the flat of his hand.

"I'm teaching her to keep her tail down so I don't have to see her, um—you know," he said with a shrug.

I burst out laughing, and told him it was anatomically unlikely that Coco would ever hold her tail like that as a default, and thought, *Gee, poor Dave is so repressed he's upset that his cat has an anus.*

Like everyone, Dave was a multi-faceted being, with wonderful as well as odd qualities. So I did what everyone does when somebody seems appealing. I said to myself, *Hey, we've all got our quirks*, tossed the idiosyncrasy aside, and focused on his intelligence, his acceptance of others, his feminism, and the fact that he was financially responsible. Not to mention, he cooked!

Dates with Dave became the bright and fun spots I anticipated every week. My father's health was declining, and as I shouldered more and more responsibility for his care, worry and exhaustion enveloped me like a fog. Let me be the first to admit that this may have skewed my perspective on many things.

Dave seemed shy, and like I said, a bit repressed. The chemistry between us wasn't strong, but it was going to grow—hell, it was growing already!

The first time we got naked together was in the hot tub at his place. Coco sat on the counter and watched us, wary of the candles glowing around the tub.

We splashed and played in the water, and I was thrilled to be there, pressed against him, playing in the bubbles, euphoria surging through my veins. We carried on a while, our arousal growing stronger.

Then he said, "The water's cooling off, we could add more hot…" but he climbed out and wrapped a blue towel neatly around his waist so he looked like a guy in the Sears catalogue, and added, "You can just finish yourself off on one of those water jets there, if you want."

Whaaat? Quick as lightning, I smoothed my face over, tipped my head, made a little half smile as if considering it, as if it was the most normal thing in the world for a lover, the first time the two of you are together, to engage in foreplay—well, what you think is foreplay—and then suggest you might want to masturbate on a water jet while he combs his hair and gets dressed.

I looked up at him, and my mind slid into a tailspin of reasoning—*there's a wide range of variation in sex practices considered normal, and beyond that, a wider range of unusual, but perfectly harmless things that are fine between consenting adults.*

I grinned like nothing could be better than this, and said, "Can I have a towel?"

I dried myself off and pressed the water out of my hair very carefully, as if these tasks required great precision. I told myself that beginnings are often awkward, and not to expect too much. I told myself that he was chilled, and that can be a problem for men, and maybe he was saving his energy for later. I wrapped myself in a towel that smelled like industrial toilet cleaner, and tried not to grimace.

When we finally did have sex, it began abruptly—truly all the foreplay had happened in the hot tub six hours prior. And he went on, and on. And *on*. I was glad the lights were off so he couldn't see my face. I wondered if he'd gotten the idea from porn that good sex is simply thrusting that goes on for a long, long time. I told myself that people are wildly different, and there's a wide range of variation, and maybe his ex-wife had a leather vagina and liked it that way.

Surely the terrible sex was due to first-time awkwardness and his repressive upbringing, which could be overcome.

We kept dating, all good and fun—long as we had our pants on and Coco had her tail down. We had a talk about sex, using the technique where you mirror back what the other person says to be sure you understood. I asked for more foreplay and affection.

He requested, "During sex, act like you're enjoying it." I repeated this back, thinking that

In the Glow of the Lavalamp

I'd be happy to show it just as soon as I was enjoying it.

Sex without love can be all right, can even be great on occasion—I've heard. But sex without desire is weird, in fact creepy. My own desire was rapidly shrinking, and I wasn't sure what was happening in Dave's head, but getting past that awkward first time hadn't really made things better. I kept telling myself there's a wide range of variation in what's normal.

Once on a road trip, in mid discussion of the pros and cons of cruise control, Dave turned to me and said, "What about anal?"

"Cruise control?"

"Sex," he said.

"Oh. You think that's a good idea?"

"Yeah. You'd like it. Since going to the bathroom feels good, it makes sense that anal sex would feel good too."

"Uh." I stalled and my stomach withdrew up into the space where my lungs should be. "I, uh. . . Well I've never thought using the bathroom feels particularly good."

"Yes it does."

"You know...here's this—during my colonoscopy two years ago they found internal hemorrhoids, and I doubt that anal sex would be a good idea, considering that."

He looked at me steady and unblinking. "You could have surgery," he said.

Damn.

"I'm not having surgery," I said. The thought that *there's a wide range of variation in sexual behavior that is considered normal* unspooled like movie music in my head. "Tell you what—let's get the vanilla stuff going nicely first." I could see that this would buy me quite a lot of time.

We got books and workbooks, we did exercises, Coco continued to hold her tail aloft, and we continued with sex that consisted of not much more than endless ramming. We used a ton of coconut oil to make this possible.

I needed to find a constructive use for the time while he was pounding away, and thought I should somehow get credit for those hours. There had to be an online university that would give me a master's degree. I was certainly putting in the time. Until I found that institution, though, I decided I would learn about the U.S. Presidents, in particular the ones we skipped over in school. During the relentless poking I could practice calling them to memory. Taft, McKinley, Cleveland…Trust-busting, the Sixteenth Amendment.

Even now, years later, the smell of coconut oil brings Chester A. Arthur's civil service reforms and his magnificent sideburns to mind.

Dave showed me a pamphlet from the Spanking Club of New York, or SCONY, which he'd picked up "in a headshop." The crease where it folded was worn soft—it was downright historic. The fact that he'd saved it fourteen years didn't faze me in the slightest—he still had a ticket stub from a 1980's Yes concert. Looking back on it though, the concert ticket was not worn soft from handling.

I kept learning more presidential history and thinking about the wide range of variation in what is normal. I'd recently bought some iolite earrings and learned the geologic term, *pleochroic*, used to describe a mineral that appears to be different colors when observed from different angles. I thought, *Aren't we all like that, in a way—reflecting a varying array of colors and characteristics when properly seen and appreciated?* Maybe I just didn't have an expansive enough perspective on my love life yet. Everything, it seemed, could be pressed into service to justify and prolong the cruise.

For Christmas, he gave me books and a beautifully wrapped mystery package. Butt beads. They looked like a baby's teething toy—bland, translucent plastic. I hid them in the dresser under my sweaters and muttered to myself about the *wide range of variation in normal sexual behavior.*

The cruise on DeNial was at its peak about then; I guess you could say I was dining at the Captain's table, drunk on my ass. Somehow I managed not to permit certain realities to peak through, like the fact that the stuff he was suggesting seemed downright grotesque in the absence of any interest in whether I was getting off or even having a tolerable time.

My friends assumed I was blissfully bedded with my sweetheart and smiled knowingly whenever they wished me a hot and happy weekend with him. I ducked my head and said, "You know, things aren't always as glorious as they appear from the outside." I said no more out of loyalty to Dave—after all, we were trying to address it weren't we? Well, yes and no—our efforts with the workbooks and exercises had fizzled out. The only nod he gave to my experience was when his erection wilted. After a number of resuscitation attempts, he turned to me and said, "Well let's make this about you, what do you want?"

Having learned the frustrating way that his attention span for "making it about you" generally lasted forty seconds, I resisted the urge to say, "Sleep." Instead, I muttered something like, "Let's just snuggle for now." The truth is, though, sleep is way better than lousy sex. Always.

I knew the fact that the sex was never good meant something was wrong, but between the enjoyment of his companionship out of bed, the shame of failing, and the fact that I was in the midst of moving my father into assisted living, it wasn't an auspicious time for staring down reality. I simply could not handle a breakup while my dad's life was breaking apart. So we continued.

As the months passed, I forged a bond with Coco, who still hadn't learned to hold her tail down. I decided to make her my ally.

I opened the package of butt beads and rubbed them with chicken grease. Most of it I wiped off, but not before making sure that some got into the little holes in the beads. The next time I went to Dave's for the weekend, the greased butt beads went with me, in a Ziploc bag.

Dave had been a vegetarian for decades, so Coco had never indulged in chicken. She quickly sniffed it out, purred, and licked the zipper on my overnight bag. I petted her and smiled.

We had the usual pounding and pounding, and I silently reviewed Woodrow Wilson's work with the National Park Service.

The next morning while Dave started the coffee, I took the butt beads out of the Ziploc and placed them under the bed. Coco was downstairs, but I had a feeling she would find them.

And she did. We were at the kitchen table, having toast and reading the paper when she darted in, the chickeny beads gripped in her teeth. I sipped my coffee and looked out the window.

Dave crumpled the paper into his lap and yelled, "Coco! What do you have? Nasty, nasty, those don't go in your *mouth*!"

Eventually this relationship came to an end, which you no doubt foresaw back in the hot tub. After a while, I got around to trying to learn from it. I chatted with a good friend, a psychologist. I told her that I'd spent about half the time I dated him trying to cover my butt, literally. We laughed. I cautiously volunteered the information that he'd wanted to hide his cat's anus.

She used a phrase I've never heard her say, before—or since: "That's so messed up."

"Yeah, it's absurd." I chuckled uneasily. "Does that mean he's just super repressed or what?"

"Well," long pause. "I've never spoken with him and don't know him," she said. "But it sounds more like an obsession and his attempt not to acknowledge it."

"What? You mean he's obsessed with his cat's—"

"I don't know that," she said. "But that's what it sounds like."

"Oooh," I said. "Oh." And the cruise ended with a crash as three hundred things fell into place.

STAYIN' ALIVE

Bobby
Age 19
April 1978

STAYIN' ALIVE

My cousin told me that getting a little bit scared on a date can be a good thing. Not life-and- death scared, but like a roller coaster, or driving by a haunted house. He said being scared is a kind of arousal or passion and could lead to other passion of the best sort. With this in mind, I planned my Saturday evening with Sheila, the most gorgeous girl in the county. She was so fine, out of my league, really.

For days now I'd been wearing out the soundtrack to *Saturday Night Fever* on my new eight-track player. Friday evening I blared it while I washed and waxed the car and thought about ghost stories I could tell Sheila. That one about the escaped convict with a hook for one arm was on my mind.

I'd made a hook out of a wire coat hanger and slipped it down between the driver's seat and the door for easy reach if a moment came when I wanted to attach it to the window or who knows what.

Two yellow packs of Juicy Fruit gum, her favorite, were in the ashtray. When she chewed it, the air around us smelled like a holiday, like those drinks in plastic coconuts, like peaches, bananas, pineapples—like fun times in a convertible. Not that I had a convertible—I had a sunroof. My ride was a 1975 silver Monte Carlo—not too shabby.

I shined my platform shoes. Those beauties—loafers in a rusty tan, with a cream-colored top piece. They looked like something the Jackson Five might've worn—not onstage, not that flashy. Maybe to negotiate their next contract.

I splashed myself with Hai Karate; chicks loved that stuff, and I kind of liked it, too. I was ready to rock in the way that only a nineteen-year-old guy with a job, a car, and a boner can be.

At the Plaza shopping center, I joined the line of cars circling through and around. On weekends, hundreds of us cruised the parking lot, so many that it backed up out onto the highway. Usually a girl would ride around the loop with me once or twice. After a while she'd get out and talk to her friends. Sometimes she'd ride with me all evening, and we'd hit the Burger Boy. On the best nights, we'd go parking.

Stayin' Alive

Sheila stood out by the Pizza Shoppe with her friends. She was hard to miss, in her purple mini-dress, her long hair all fluttery. She'd cruised the plaza with me before, but that was all.

My heart did a little stuttery thing, and I put a hand on it. "Easy there, easy now," I said.

I pushed my sunglasses up on my head so they swept back the wings on my hair and gave me that look like I'd just come off a motorcycle. I waved at her.

When she got in my car, she brought a cloud of Jovan Musk oil and shampoo, really fresh and sweet—it mixed in kind of nice with my cologne. She was a fox, her dress hitting high on those tan, smooth legs. Yikes. I wanted to slide my hand under that silky dress and squeeze her, but I just smiled and kept my hands to myself.

She flashed her big brown eyes. "Que pasa?"

"Que pasa, baby?" I said. "How you doing?"

The September evening was right on the edge between warm and cool—perfect weather really, but I was sweating. I'd not been with anybody as fine as her before. In fact, I'd only ever been with one girl, and it didn't go great. Don't get me wrong. It wasn't bad. Well, it was close to bad. I didn't really know exactly what I was doing.

I'd been reading up on the subject, though. I found a copy of *The Sensuous Man* in my cousin's garage. That book about had it covered, I tell you. Stuff it might have taken me a long time to figure out on my own, like special stuff you could do with your tongue. Between that book and the info from my cousin about getting scared, I was set. And come to think of it, a little scared was exactly how my stomach felt. So all I had to do was get her a little bit scared like I was.

We stopped for burgers and headed down by the river to eat. Sheila held the bag, the toasty, greasy smell rolling off the fries while I drove, *Saturday Night Fever* blaring, the BeeGees singing high, so high. I never did get it, those words about the *New York Times'* effect on man, but I didn't care. That music had an urgency to it just like I was feeling—like something important was about to happen. Soon.

Sheila's cloth purse jangled, sounded like it was full of keychains and plastic baubles. It was big enough to hold a couple of footballs.

"What you got in there?" I asked.

"I'm not telling," she said, and winked at me.

I got the shivers. Flecks of light bounced off the little disco ball hanging from the mirror and danced across us, making it seem like everything was in motion.

I figured I'd get started with a ghost story and asked if she knew the one about the escaped convict with a hook on his arm. A good one, because he was sneaking up on a couple getting some loving in their car—kind of nudged the mind in the direction I hoped we were going.

"Oh yeah," she said. "Everybody knows that story about the hook man."

A small setback. There were other ghost stories. Hell. I'd make one up if I had to, about a ghost that comes around rocking and tipping cars if the people in them are wearing too many clothes. That made me laugh.

"What's funny?" she asked.

I shook my head. "Stupid ghost stories Dwayne told me. Who'd believe that about the guy with a hook anyways?" I looked at her hands. "You got a new ring?"

"Yeah. It's a mood ring. Changes color depending how I feel."

"Neat," I said. "So it's baby blue right now—what does that mean?"

"Means I'm happy. And hungry."

I reached over and squeezed her leg right above the knee. "That's good to hear, baby doll."

She giggled and fiddled with the ring, opened the bag and pulled out some fries, put one in her mouth, and one in mine. She touched my lips with her fingers and I almost slammed on the brakes right there in the middle of the road.

At the river, we fed each other more French fries between bites of burgers. Every time I put a fry in her mouth I made sure to touch her face or shoulder. The book said it was important to show affection to make her want you. The sun was going down, and she was such a fox, I wanted to slide that dress right off her shoulders, push her down on the rocks, and kiss her. But I stayed beside her and kept chewing my burger, thinking about her tan lines.

Other couples settled in around us. Cars were everywhere, practically bumper to bumper by the time we finished eating. This was not what I had in mind. How could I pull the hook out with people all around us? Besides, Sheila was special, and there was nothing romantic about a parking lot, even if it was by the river. Leave that to the high school kids.

"Kinda crowded here," I said, glancing at her face, which was getting pink. "You want to stay here or would you rather go somewhere more private?"

She smiled. "Well, maybe a little more private."

The hairs on my arm stood up like a parade marching on my skin or something. I checked the mood ring and it was still baby blue.

The eight-track was on "More than a Woman" as we drove away.

What could be more than a woman? I wondered. Not much that I could think of.

"There's an old graveyard down off Yellow Creek Road, we could try that," I said.

Her face lit up. "Oooooh, spooky, yeah."

We rode with the sunroof open and a warm breeze washing over us as darkness fell.

The Waverly Cemetery had two parts. One side where the dates on tombstones went back over a hundred years, even to the Civil War. On the modern side, two of the graves were so recent the grass hadn't grown back over the red clay yet—seemed harsh and a little creepy. I parked under a tree by a big metal trashcan overflowing with stuff that used to be on the graves, I guess—baskets, ribbons, green spongy blocks for sticking flowers in. Fake poinsettias were on top and a few had come apart with red petals scattered on the ground, like giant drops of blood in the headlight beams.

Sheila unwrapped a fresh piece of gum and popped it in her mouth.

I stared at her lips as she chewed.

"You want one?" she asked, holding the package out.

The mood ring looked kind of greenish in the twilight. I thought it was probably a good sign.

"I want one of these." I leaned in for a kiss. I could taste the gum, sweet and fruity, as I sank my hands into her silky hair. "You smell so good."

"Mmmm," she said around the kiss and pulled away and took out her chewing gum.

And then I broke out in a sweat, and the bottom of my stomach dropped out, like it fell down a well, with a dull pain.

"Dang," I said, "I hate to break the moment, but I think I'm gonna go see a man about a dog before we get started here."

She laughed. "You better not pee on a grave!"

"I won't. Ghosts'll come after you if you do that."

I closed the car door gently and looked around. A dry leaf skittered across in front of the car making a sound like *scththh*. Something felt like a feather brushing the back of my neck. I clapped a hand there while I looked for a place to go. A stone wall ran around the cemetery, and outside that were brambles and woods. I could go in those bushes, but I'd be taking down my pants and begging three thousand ticks, chiggers, and mosquitoes to join the party. It was dark; maybe I could get away with squatting down behind one of those big husband-and-wife deals with their names side by side. I couldn't see Sheila in the car, and I hoped she couldn't see me. I didn't want to desecrate a grave, but I had to go, and soon.

My lower belly seized up, and I hopped over the stone wall, brambles crunching under my shoes. I couldn't see the ground and hoped to God no snakes were back there. Something itchy was on my hand as I undid my belt and went low.

When it was over, I snuck back through the graveyard, my shoes going *chuff chuff* in the grass. I stayed away from those newer burials where the grass hadn't grown back. Those could be people you'd met before, or even stood behind in line at Kmart.

"Did the hook man come after you?" asked Sheila.

"Not yet." I opened the window. "It's a really nice night out there. Let's get some air."

We put the seats back a bit and settled in. She was kissing on my neck right where it joins the collarbone on one side, and I swear nothing had ever felt better. I tried to return the favor and was doing the same to her when my stomach had a pain again.

"Dadgummit," I said. "I hate this, but I've got to go again."

"Is something wrong?"

"Nah, just bad timing." When I opened the car door, the coat hanger hook stuck out, right there in the light; I shoved it way back behind the seat. "I'll be quick. You stay where you are, don't move." What in the world was wrong with me? Nerves? Bad food? I couldn't tell.

I went to the older side of the cemetery this time and climbed over the stone wall where the woods weren't too thick. My shoes sank into the earth. It was darker away from the gravestones, and that was mostly good, but it worried me that I couldn't see what was back there, including the stuff I uprooted to wipe my butt.

As my eyes adjusted to the darkness I saw there were graves out here, too, little flat markers in the ground. That kind of got to me. It was like I couldn't escape them. I climbed back over the wall and headed toward the car. Small stones, about the size of license plates, stuck up out of the ground like scattered teeth in an old man's mouth. I tripped over one and almost went down. The platform shoes were not really a plus at that point.

In the car, Sheila was brushing her hair. "You all right?" she asked.

The mood ring was sort of gray.

"Yeah," I said. "I think I'm good now."

"We could go for a walk." She peered out the window.

"Heck no. I want to be here with you—I really like the way you kiss." I poked her in the ribs gently. "Besides, it's spooky out there."

We got back to kissing, always a good thing. The third time I had to go, I crouched down and duck-walked over to the trashcan, staying under the line of sight from the car, and was going to grab some of those fake flowers, because they were made of cloth or something and might make good toilet paper. But I couldn't get them out of the trash without standing up, and Sheila might notice. So I took the petals on the ground, thinking how dirty they probably were. Something howled in the darkness, maybe a dog, maybe a coyote.

The wind tossed tree branches up high and the leaves slithered against each other like somebody whispering. When I stepped on a twig and it snapped, I jumped and caught myself on a crooked old stone with blurry writing: "Gone but not forgotten," and some other stuff I couldn't read. It came to me that I might be too scared for it to be a help with romance.

I was beginning to despair of ever making Sheila mine. If I could just get ten uninterrupted minutes in the car with her, I knew I could do it. Maybe even eight minutes, or seven. But every time I came back from a bathroom break we had to start over, building the mood. The book said you have to go slow and build up to it or the girl will shut you down.

She looked bored when I came back.

"You know," I said, "this place is starting to give me the creeps. Maybe we need a change of scenery. You think we might be better off at that construction site off Walkup Road where the old Pegram place used to be? Nobody'll be down there tonight."

She smiled and tipped her head. "Wow! There used to be a graveyard at Walkup Road, too. A little one. They dug it up and moved the graves so they could build houses."

"Really?"

"Uh huh," she said. "Some people think it's haunted." She put a hand on my arm, her eyes wide, mouth twitching. "Oh come on, are you that scared?" She looked deep in my eyes and grabbed my knee. "Was a ghost out there? What happened?"

"You happened." I kissed her. "We'll stay here."

The moon was up high by then, spilling silver all over everything.

She was quiet, and I couldn't see the mood ring.

"Come here. You're not scared, are you?" I asked. I put the tape deck on low. "Don't be scared. Ghosts don't like music; they won't bother us."

"You're the one who wanted to leave," she said.

"Heck no, I don't want to leave! I could stay here all night with you."

Slowly, my stomach calmed and we settled into a good make-out session.

The tape was playing "Night Fever," which pretty well described the moment for us. We teased and squeezed each other, and the tension went up fast, in a good way. We took off a few clothes. Finally, she straddled me. She had a fairly slight build and so did I, so it wasn't much trouble to get in the proper position. She seemed to know exactly what to do.

At last! It felt so good I decided I probably loved her. I wanted to be with her like this forever. I'd have agreed to anything; I would have married her, even married her in a graveyard, but all she seemed to want was to continue on. "You're beautiful," I said.

"Uhhhhhh," she said.

Because of the way we were situated, her head was moving with our rhythm, to where it was sticking out of the sunroof. I let the seat back more in case she didn't want to keep popping out the roof. Still she kept on, so I guess she liked it. I wanted to finish quick, before something else happened, even though *The Sensuous Man* said it was better if you take your time and go slow. Right away though—I mean we'd barely got going—she tensed up something fierce, and her legs clinched alongside me, hard—so tight around me I could barely move.

Damn, I'm doing good! I thought. The book had talked a lot about how you have to build things up, and it takes longer for the girl.

It seemed really fast for her to be having a climax, and I hurried to catch up. She screamed out my name, and I said, "Yeah, baby!"

Then she screamed again. "It's choking me!"

The sunroof had closed up tight against her neck. I grabbed for the switch under her leg behind me to open it, and it wouldn't work. My hand scrambled on the coat hanger hook. It was stuck in the console, jamming the switch. I twisted it out and hit the button hard. Finally the roof opened. Sheila fell back against the door. I stuffed the hanger under the seat and made a big deal that the switch was jammed under her leg, like that had been the whole problem.

"Are you OK?" I asked, trying to get a look at her neck.

"I guess," she said, keeping a hand on her throat. "What was that wire doing back there?"

"Gosh, I don't know. Just some old coat hanger in the back. Is your neck all right?"

"I want to see that wire thing." She pulled herself away from me.

I groped behind me, tried to unbend the hooked end, and slowly handed her the hanger.

"What the hell is this supposed to be?"

"A hook," I said, my head down. "I thought it would make things exciting. I guess it hit the roof switch and jammed it. I'm sorry." Then, with a little chuckle, I asked, "Did you come?"

She didn't laugh. The mood ring had gone dark, like the cinders on a half-burned log.

She reached for her underwear. "Can I have a little privacy here?"

I stepped out of the car, tucked in, buckled up, and looked off into the darkness, where I could barely see the trees. It seemed I would not be getting off either.

After a while, she put her seat back up, and I heard her rattling the purse.

"You OK?" I asked again.

"I guess so," she said. "I'm still alive."

"And I'm glad you are." The book said nothing about somebody almost getting beheaded by a sunroof, and I had no idea what to do.

I took her back to the Plaza, and she slammed the car door hard when she got out. The fringe on her purse caught; she opened the door, pulled the purse free, and then slammed it again. She walked off toward the Pizza Shop and didn't even say good night.

OK STUPID

Alice
Age 52
March 2012

OK STUPID

I set sail with high hopes and two vast areas of ignorance: 1. what online dating is like in middle age, and 2. what an oddity I am. As a politically liberal, fairly tall, never-married, non-religious, over-educated female, I qualified for the label "weird." I didn't know that early on—I assumed everybody was a lot like me, maybe a bit less shy.

Men, men, men! It was exhilarating to have guys email me out of the blue. Some sites were free! What did I have to lose? Optimism can be more perspective-skewing than huffing bath salts.

I'd spent a good bit of time on my own profile and user name, trying to succinctly convey the essence of who I am, emphasizing strong points. I couldn't wait to see what the guys brought. Well! How was I to choose among LongdickSam, BigDick42, Goldenass, Supercock, and JuicyBits69? I moved on to HogHunter58 and Harley Stud 4U, hoping for a bit of depth. Never mind the names—surely the profiles had more substance. One fellow noted that if he still had a full head of hair, then it wasn't necessary for him to have a job. Some sent pictures of their privates. Others gave advice on dating a smoker, monogamy, my appearance, sex life, views on civil rights, and the appropriate role for Jesus in my life.

A few said they had Asperger's Syndrome and wore it proudly like a merit badge. One fellow assured me that he was "self-centered, as most musicians are." Another stated that he was "an uncompromising man" as if that made him more appealing.

Billy had memorized *all* the Psalms and was working on Proverbs. Although I was initially taken aback, the more I thought about it, the more I wanted to meet him to see how he used those in daily life. We never met though—he thought science was a conspiracy, and I work in a lab.

Richard wanted to wear a ruffly dress and be put on a collar and leash. What the hell was I supposed to do with him once he was on the leash? Well, since pulling his weight in the kitchen is the best thing a guy can do to impress me, I figured hell yeah, that's fine if he wants to wear a dog collar and a party dress—I'll just tie his leash where he can reach both the dishwasher and the sink.

My first date from online stood me up. At the time I was profoundly grateful. I'd worked myself into a frenzy, gone to the coffeehouse filled with anxiety and dread, gotten my tea, and sat there, and sat there. After waiting twenty minutes, I left, limp with relief. Only upon receiving his email the next day, did I get mad. "I forgot about meeting you, fell asleep. Sorry if it may have caused any inconvenience..."

Really? If it may have caused any inconvenience? Heavens no, I often try on twelve outfits, fuss over my makeup, drive twenty-five minutes, stress to the point I dip the belt to my coat in the toilet, and then sit, staring into space. No inconvenience at all. But I'd been spared meeting him, which was lovely.

Allen, who I'd met briefly in high school, invited me for a meal at his home, or hoarding den. We had to turn sideways to navigate through stacks of newspapers. The kitchen floor sagged dangerously on one side, and he warned me, "Don't walk there!" Halfway through a lovely dinner of sea bass and asparagus, he looked at me intently and said, "Do you have to go to the bathroom?"

I said, "No," very casually as if people frequently asked me that over dinner on a first date, as if I were not terrified that he was going to suggest some weird sex act.

"If you do, I can show you where the bathroom is," he said.

"Great!"

Joe, I met for Indian food. He told me that his dad—whom he lived with and would see again in three hours—had a prostate issue, and he wanted to check in with him. Over dinner, he made the call. While shoveling his curry down, he asked if Dad had pain, what a corrective procedure might involve, and whether there was a discharge, which there must have been, since he asked if it was foul-smelling. Right there at the table. At that point, I gave myself permission to quit trying to make it a pleasant evening, quit trying to sustain conversation (when he wasn't on the phone), quit trying to be friendly—simply quit.

We said goodbye, and I walked to my car. The air was sweet and cool, and the breeze tossed my hair. I felt my muscles bite down as I climbed the steep hill to my parking spot. My heart rose with the wind; it was the best part of the date.

I became skilled at translating key phrases in men's profiles. "Age is just a number" means *I generally date people young enough to be my grandchildren.* "No Drama!" means *I tend to stir up a lot of unpleasant stuff and if you react, then you carry the blame for everything.* "Looking for a slender woman" means *I may have a gut the size of Montana, but you're supposed to look like a model.*

Some guys, actually still married, were shocked that I found this an obstacle to dating them. The most common explanation:

"That marriage is *done*; you can stick a fork in it." I imagined myself in a chef's hat, stabbing something with a giant fork. One still-married man seethed with rage when I said no thanks. He said that since I'd never been married I had no business on a dating site, and that it was clear I knew nothing about relationships, and was probably a baby killer. The intensity of his anger frightened me. I wanted to flee, but I'd heard the website never deleted your profile even when your subscription ended, so I changed mine up. I was now a turquoise-eyed, eight-foot-tall, bald–headed Buddhist, age ninety-two, headlined by, "Age is just a number."

Within twenty-four hours my account was shut down, even though I still had a month left on my membership. Shame overwhelmed me. I'd never heard of anyone being kicked off a dating site. Not only was I probably a relationship idiot, but my gentle eight-foot, turquoise-eyed, Buddhist self wasn't fit to participate in the game. I thought there was someone for everyone.

The lesson here was not to take things personally, and I won't further embarrass myself by divulging how long that took to sink in.

Eventually, I moved on to a free site and soon had a promising first date with Romeo. All good, except at the end he commanded, "Email me your phone number." I decided to overlook this since he'd spent years in the corporate world and no doubt had confused me with one of his minions. When he asked for a second date, I cheerfully met him at a lodge, where we played with a dog outside. When we went in for dinner, I said I wanted to wash the dog off my hands and headed to the restroom. Upon my return, he was nowhere in sight, so I sat in the lobby and waited. As the minutes ticked by, I imagined he was having some *problem*, and worked up a good deal of sympathy, thinking how awful it would be to have an attack of GI distress on a date. Poor Romeo. Ten minutes passed. I was thinking of sending another gentleman in to check on him when he popped out of the dining area, and said, "Where've you been? C'mon, I've got us a table!"

Not only had he found a table, but he'd found the buffet, filled his plate, and begun eating. I got a plate and joined him. He spoke at length about his real estate investments. The meal was marred only by him jumping in front of me to get at the peach cobbler on the dessert bar. It was almost like a hockey move the way he wielded that long-handled spoon and angled himself.

Finally the check arrived and he said, "I guess we'd better go." With that he walked rapidly away from the table, leaving me with the bill and my astonishment that he had depths of rudeness yet unplumbed. What else might manifest before I got to my car? I grabbed the check and followed him to the cashier, where I plunked down a credit card.

Romeo watched and said, "Are you sure?"

I almost laughed. I'd never been more sure of anything in my life—sure that I was done here. I'm all for sharing expenses and also big on discussing it. I nodded with a grim smile. As we walked to my car, I could see an attempt at a kiss coming. He leaned over to deliver it, and at the last second I turned my face away, so he awkwardly pecked my cheek. If I'd had a hockey stick I'd have put the peach cobbler block on him.

Fortunately, hope is not a logical thing. After many disasters, I found a guy whose weirdness was counterpart to mine. The first time he came to my place for dinner, we cooked it together. Then he told me to take a break while he cleaned the kitchen. No party dress, no collar—he just cleaned the kitchen.

THE BATTLE BELOW THE CLOUDS

Lucinda
Age 45
October, 2008

THE BATTLE BELOW THE CLOUDS

I tried to date a Republican once.

All my life I'd been surrounded by liberals, and online dating at middle-age ushered in a new era for me. At first, I simply hinted at where I fell on the political spectrum, thinking that men who were far to the right would prefer to seek similar partners. Oh no. Many forged ahead, saying generous things like, "I can respect your views, so I think you should be able to respect mine."

Yeah. I should be OK with their views that anybody who is not a guy—a white, straight, Christian guy, in fact—should have fewer rights than they do.

Usually I made excuses. Always I said no.

Once the national divide between the political parties became particularly fierce and bizarre, I found myself intolerant in an ugly way. Not liking what I saw in myself, I decided it was time to be less judgmental and that I should just try dating a Republican. So

In the Glow of the Lavalamp

when the next conservative guy asked me out, rather than dismiss him, I mentioned in an offhand way that I thought we had rather different political views.

"That's OK," he said. "I think if you let me have a chance, I could talk you out of it and make you see my side."

Really? I found him a bit naïve, but I sent a smiley-faced email saying, "We'll see about that."

He replied with a missive about the Gay Pedophile Agenda—as if it was a recognized plan, like the Kiwanis Club Agenda, or Mothers Against Drunk Driving. I remained calm and gently tried to feed him a few facts about the demographics of pedophiles— straight white guys, mostly. Again, he confidently stated that given enough time, he could convince me. I told myself he was probably just over-protective of his kindergarten-age daughter and suggested we move on to other topics.

He finally asked me out after a lengthy email flirtation, during which it became clear that we would do best to avoid a number of subjects, including, but not limited to: climate change, the Bible, the President, civil rights, Hurricane Katrina, gay people, doctors, taxes, the FDA, and energy-efficient light bulbs. He specified that he wanted to spend no money on the date and not go anywhere that he wouldn't want to go anyhow, so that no time or money was wasted.

I felt so special.

He suggested we meet at a Civil War battlefield site, now a park with a little museum. His email said he'd be in an F-150 FWD, which made as much sense to me as if he'd said he'd be riding in R2D2, or WD40. For the unschooled, it's a big truck. High up off the ground. High up enough so you're almost in another level of the atmosphere, above the clouds, even.

I told myself that he was a *history buff*, not a Civil War fanatic. He knew all about the war, which battle, when and where, which commander, flanks, reconnoitering, all that. I wondered at the mass slaughter and tried to let the details fly over my head. Some people say the war was about states' rights, but to me it boiled down to the economy, which in the South was based on slave labor. I saw it as a national shame that the war had to be fought at all. I know that the Americans weren't the first to own slaves, nor would we be the last. Still I found it horrifying. Thus began the glory of our first date—not a ritual, exactly, but a sort of reverent immersion of ourselves in the history of the conflict.

Apparently, in the battle that took place on this site, the site of our first date, the Generals on both sides had used the same strategy; attack the right flank and cut off lines of supply and escape. I complimented my date on his vast battle knowledge and asked a lot of questions.

We flirted and walked the ground where men had shot and bayoneted each other. He took my hand in the "Slaughter Pen." I flashed him a smile and tried not to imagine the carnage of soldiers and horses around us.

After we'd been walking for an hour or two, he turned to me with a grin. "Want to go sit in the truck and catch your breath?"

I said sure.

The cursive Ford logo on the truck gleamed in a wholesome way. I felt like a child climbing up into the cab and wondered how his five-year-old daughter got in. The tires were huge with deep tread, like teeth ready to bite down on mud or gravel.

The back seat was midget-sized, but up front, two St. Bernards could've sat at my feet. The navy blue dash shined like he'd Armoralled it; not a bit of lint speckled the floor. Sitting up high gave me a sense of freedom and possibility, and somehow that was funny and thrilling, like being at the circus.

We chatted on about the battlefield, the graveyard nearby, and the age of the trees now growing all around us. After a bit he said, "I'm going to kiss you now," and pulled me close.

The man could kiss like a million bucks. Like two million bucks, really, or six. I mean I saw stars and heard choirs. The blood-soaked ground beneath us faded to oblivion, and his gay pedophile agenda flew away out the open windows of the F-150, into the bright October sky. And like the zip zap of a lightning strike, being tolerant became fabulous.

We kissed until I felt like I was going to catch fire right there in the cab of the truck at 3:30 in the afternoon in the Civil War parking lot with tourists coming and going around us. It was delightful, and probably more so because it was unexpected.

When a family came to get in the car next to us, I pushed back from him, grinning like a fool, and rested against the door.

He smiled and put a hand on my knee. "Well, we've taken this about as far as we can," he said.

I nodded, and bit back the words, "What makes you think that?"

I collected my purse, and climbed down from the F-150.

He kissed me goodbye once more at my car. "I'm not going to do much, 'cause there's kids right over there."

"Good idea," I said.

Beaming and buzzing on my way home, I damn near crashed my car, slamming on the brakes and leaving rubber on the road when I came up on some stalled vehicles on the interstate. When I got going again, I drove horribly and fast, trying to escape the reach of his pheromones.

I was beginning to think that dating across party lines might have some possibility after all. I had dated enough liberal men to know that they came with their own sets of drawbacks. That, however, is another story.

We continued to make eyes at each other via email. I side-stepped any political discussions that might cloud my rose-colored glasses. He had an every-other-weekend custody arrangement with his daughter, so there was no rush to schedule the next date.

When he asked me, I had to tell him sorry, no.

I wanted to see him. But I had a colonoscopy coming up, and with the two weekend days needed to prepare for it, I would not be leaving the house. I had no intention of telling him about this. But what the hell was I going to tell him? I tried to come up with something believable that also reflected favorably on me, like working on a Habitat house. I lectured myself about how this relationship should be built on honesty. Finally, I just told him I was having a colonoscopy and said how scared I was about it.

He told me not to worry, that he was going to email me something that might help.

I swooned. I'd never dated anybody so thoughtful. His email:

Although slightly morbid, here's something I suspect will not only take your mind off things, it may well bolster your spirits and give you a measure of comfort. It isn't much certainly, but I'm hoping you'll accept and enjoy my simple gift in the spirit in which it was intended. And if you have seen it prior, then perhaps try reading it once again that you may draw strength from it.

It's a famous letter written by a Civil War soldier to his wife, on the eve of the battle in which he was killed. It's not every day we are privy to a man's private thoughts as he contemplates his likely demise in such a courageous and noble fashion. And we would do well when we face critical moments in life to follow this example. For it's those pivotal moments and how we handle them that define our character, and ultimately, define us.

Then followed the historic letter, which did indeed serve as a distraction. In flowery nineteenth-century language, the solider bid his wife and life farewell as he foresaw his imminent death, maiming, or dismemberment. It was both poignant and hilariously inappropriate.

I survived the colonoscopy (faced it valiantly), and we got our second date on the books. The drive-in movies. I wondered if he now saw me as a good investment and planned to pay for the date. Being the prudent sort, I brought cash.

We were to meet at a post office and leave my car there. I arrived early, which is what I do when I'm nervous. While waiting for him, I texted my friends and developed a serious case of anxiety farts, which is another thing I do when I'm nervous. These farts have no odor to speak of, but they are quite loud, kind of like popcorn popping.

My friends were more amused than I was.

One replied, "OMG, I'm so glad I'm married."

Yeah, I thought, how nice for you.

The F-150 gleamed when he swung into the parking lot, grinning, and way cuter than I had remembered. I climbed up into the truck. Since it was supposed to be a cool-ish night, I wore a bulky cotton turtleneck sweater, which was about as sexy as everything else in the LL Bean catalog. At home in the mirror, the brilliant blue color of it had seemed attractive, but as soon as I got in the truck, I knew it was a mistake. The day was still warm, and I was sweating like a pig. I picked at the cord that ran across the vinyl truck seat while he drove.

The late afternoon sun still shone when we got to the drive-in. He paid, while I looked on and wondered what I would be paying. We parked and sat uncomfortably, staring at the screen and making small talk as the ads for refreshments went by. Why was I here, sweating in the sun, wearing a bulky turtleneck, with a Tea-Party-type guy who hated to spend money on a date unless he knew it was a sure thing? At that moment I'd have paid a large sum to be at home, in sweats and a T-shirt, alone.

Finally, twilight, and the movie started. We studied the film as if our lives depended upon catching every nuance. Clouds covered the moon, and I was grateful beyond words when darkness tucked around us. I sat very still, lest my butt make another loud noise, and when it did, I talked loudly, trying to mask the sound. He smiled.

We watched and watched the movie, a current-events-related drama, and I wondered if he still liked me, because he didn't even try to hold my hand, and why else were we at the drive-in, for heaven's sake? I was too stiff to move even a centimeter toward him, so I continued to stare at the movie and kept one hand on the seat, available for holding. He ignored it. Maybe by now he hated me and my liberal views, my shallow understanding of the Civil War, and my giant sweater. The whole endeavor seemed like a stupid charade.

Movie One ended. He ate his hotdog and sipped his Coke. I nibbled a few pieces of popcorn. We got settled in for Movie Two, a Bollywood-meets-Mean-Girls type thing, less interesting than Movie One.

Finally, he put a hand up across the back of the seat and played with my hair. I jumped.

Somehow we got to kissing and sitting closer, and oddly, it was not nearly as thrilling as it had been in the same truck in broad daylight at the Civil War Battlefield. Who'd have thought that was a turn-on?

After a while, the kissing made us more relaxed. And it got marginally better. We completely ignored Movie Two and talked and kissed.

"I'm attracted to you," he said, reaching for the zipper on my jeans. "It's baffling."

"Um, what?" I said, placing my forearm directly on the zipper so it couldn't be moved.

"I like trashy women," he said, his face glowing in the reflection of the screen. "You know that song, 'Trashy Women'?"

"Yeah," I said. "I know it, 'Too much lipstick, too much rouge, Gets me excited, leaves me feeling confused...'"

"That's it," he said. "Like in the song, that's the kind of woman I go for, so this is radical." He gestured toward me. "For some reason I can't explain, I find you attractive." He went for the zipper again.

I bit back a retort and almost laughed out loud. Who does that? Makes a move on somebody while telling her he's baffled that he finds her attractive?

So he liked slutty-looking women? I am more the type frequently mistaken for a librarian. I routed him away from my zipper.

His hands looked very strong and kind of small, with the fingers slightly shorter than the palm. I couldn't help imagining those burly little hands groping butts with jeans so tight the rhinestone studs hurt the wearer.

I enjoyed kissing him, although being trapped in the F-150 with someone so confused about wanting to touch me had its limitations.

I repeatedly denied him access to the zipper and goods beneath it, and we settled into some advance, fend-off, and retreat that some might even call a skirmish. When he unzipped his own pants, I suppressed a shriek and wished for Dorothy's ruby slippers. He suggested we go to my house; I said no.

Back at the post office, he asked if I wanted to climb in the teeny back seat of his truck and kiss a little bit more. Knowing I would never see (or kiss) him again, I said OK and squeezed in.

The evening had grown chilly, and at last I was glad of my unattractive sweater.

"Your hair is a mess," he said.

I stifled the urge to ask, "Does it make you more baffled?"

We covered ourselves with a dusty serape-type blanket he had behind the seat, and my mind went roaming. I wondered how many women with hair-sprayed bouffants and fake eyelashes had been groped under the serape, or worse, bedded on it. I wondered if I would feel sexier if I'd worn heavy Cleopatra eyeliner, gloppy red lip gloss, and a push-up bra visible under a tight, shiny polyester shirt. I thought about why I'd never done these things and I considered their merits. It was exhausting.

Part of me, or part of my hormones at least, still wanted this far-right, big-hair-loving, baffled guy to like me.

I was stiff and creaky from folding myself into the tiny back seat, and we had lost the urgency that makes it possible to endure all kinds of awkwardness. Musing on my shortcomings as a tart had drained the fun out of it for me, and my librarian-looking self was ready to make the break and cut out for home.

I thanked him and said, "It was lots of fun."

He said he'd email.

Driving home, I felt half insane; what in the world had I just spent six hours doing? I slowly came back to myself and slumped with relief.

Days later, I was still puzzling over the experience. My attraction to him was confounding. What had charmed me? Certainly not his values or smooth mojo. Was it the F-150? Was it his complete lack of insight, and pure animal nature? Yeah, it was baffling. Maybe I liked trashy men. Maybe I'd been doing the same thing he was. Maybe tolerance and respect could be better embraced without actually embracing anyone.

OBLIGATED

Grace
Age 22
October 1983

OBLIGATED

Blake and I met at a party when we were in grad school. I was in social work, he was in geography. When he called me later, I was surprised—we hadn't seemed to hit it off that much—but I wasn't seeing anyone, and he seemed smart. I yearned to join the world of the happily coupled—ached might be a better word, in fact. So I focused on the things we had in common—hiking, beer, parties, making out.

He lived in a big house near campus, dubbed "The Fun House," with six or twelve, or maybe thirty people. The kitchen was always greasy, and the living room sat under a film of grey from years of smokers. The landlord kicked them all out—claimed he needed to remodel—but probably he was tired of renting to students who left the windows open and brought in stray dogs. I was glad. Blake seemed a bit too interested in Rosemary, one of the Fun inhabitants.

Blake had a place to move, but it wouldn't be ready for a month or two. He slept on the sofas of various friends for a week, and gradually began staying over at my apartment more and more. Then he asked if he could put some suitcases and stuff in my storage unit. I said sure, and surged with pride that at last somebody had chosen me—somebody wanted to live with me, even if only for a short time. Now everyone would think of us as Grace and Blake—a couple! We'd dated less than two months and were having fun. The sex was occasionally good, but nothing of substance had been spoken between us. Yet.

Everyone around me seemed happily ensconced with their soulmate, and I wanted that, too. My brothers, still wild and young, had each lived with a partner, but both seemed equally content with having occasional girlfriends. My sister had been married a few years, and in the condescending way of the smugly partnered and slightly scared, told me that her glorious marital state was due to good fortune in birth order. She said that our parents had been so troubled and burdened by their own lousy upbringings that there hadn't been enough love, attention, and good parenting to go around. As the eldest, she'd gotten the best they had to offer, and I'd gotten the leftovers from that, and our younger brothers had gotten the dregs. So she, the eldest, was the only one able to form a healthy, lasting relationship, while the rest of us stumbled along, romantically crippled.

At the time, I bought her theory, signed on for more therapy, ever more therapy, and from a distance, coveted her splendid marriage. I wished that I were emotionally healthy and stable enough, and appealing enough, for some guy to choose me.

I had dated my share of guys, had long-term boyfriends, some for years, but none had been inclined to cohabit with me. So when Blake bluntly asked for my key to make himself a copy, although I acted nonchalant, I was quietly ecstatic. Never mind that I didn't know him well, we didn't talk a great deal, and he still seemed to harbor some tender attachment to Rosemary.

One Friday at happy hour, too broke to spring for dinner, I was buying my own beers and Blake was buying his—we were there as a couple, but oh so independent. Rosemary breezed in the door, all glowy from the late October air, and his face lit up. They hugged, and he insisted she come sit by him. I smiled a lot and waved at her.

"I'm so hungry!" said Rosemary, like this was something we weren't all experiencing at 5:30 on a Friday.

Blake looked at her with concern, waved the waitress over, and bought her an order of French fries.

"Awww," said Rosemary, and turned toward me. "Is this guy sweet, or what?"

I nodded. "The sweetest." I excused myself to the ladies' room. This was a big damn deal. None of us could afford to eat out. We used our money for beer. And still, he'd bought her food.

When I returned, a plate of steaming fries was in front of Rosemary, and Blake was watching her salt and pepper them. The toasty, potatoey scent circled around the table. Blake handed her the ketchup with a knowing smile, and she put way too much on them.

Was this some kind of ritual they'd shared at the Fun House? I couldn't tear my eyes away from watching her put each one in her mouth.

If I'd allowed myself to think about it, I might have realized that in our near-moneyless state, buying someone food was more of a commitment than living together, especially if living together simply meant making a key to someone's apartment and showing up there each night to shower and sleep. I sipped my beer and took a big gulp of Blake's when he went to the bathroom.

In the big picture, I was happy having a live-in boyfriend. I went through the day more confident, with a spring in my step, knowing that Blake would come home to my place that evening. He didn't offer to split the rent or utilities. We never discussed it at all.

Obligated

Those thoughts flitted through my brain. I batted them away like mosquitoes, and replaced them with, *I'm living with someone! Of course there are parts of this that feel strange—it's all new to me.* I was finally less alone.

I bubbled along, and when I told my friend Alan at school, he frowned and said, "I don't think that's such a good idea."

I knew he was probably jealous of the coupledom, as people often are, and I shrugged it off.

He continued, "Grace, he's a Republican."

"So what?" I said. "It's not like I'm running for office."

"It's important," said Alan. "It means he wants war and cares more about big business than people."

"Nobody really wants war," I said.

"Has he paid rent?"

"What is this, the Inquisition? He's only been there a few days, and not at the beginning of a month. He'll offer to pay half when it comes time to pay," I said, hoping it was true.

I tossed aside Alan's petty sniping, and carried on with my now upbeat life. I'd never had an upbeat life before.

Blake called me from a football game one night and asked if I wanted to come meet him there. This was just like, *just like* half a couple calling home to check in with the partner. I had no interest in sports, and declined the invitation, but loved being called, loved him checking in with me. Clearly, I was made for the partnered life.

Later that evening when he came in from the ball game, I beamed at him and reveled in the image of both us returned to our little nest for the evening. I took my shower, and in an attempt to avoid hogging the bathroom, I sat in my bedroom afterwards, in my nightgown, combing out my wet hair.

But Blake wasn't concerned with bathroom time. He sat on the bed, took his shoes off, glanced my way, and said, "Well, I guess this is as bad as it gets, you with wet hair in your granny gown."

The air was instantly sucked out of my partnered balloon. My ribs hurt, like maybe I'd sprained them washing my hair. I went back in the bathroom, closed the door, brushed my teeth, and looked at myself in the mirror. I'd thought my nightgown was romantic. It was white cotton eyelet, like a chemise from the 1800s, but free from all the other layers. I thought this was part of living together—people take showers, their hair gets wet. Blake occasionally had wet hair, too—what was wrong with that?

I stayed in the bathroom a long time, and when I came out, he was in bed with the light off. I told myself that all couples have disagreements, and there was much for me to learn about living together. I slid into bed, keeping far to my side, and hoped I'd be able to fall asleep.

To my surprise, he reached for me. Maybe I wasn't so repulsive after all, with my wet hair, and cotton gown. Before long, we were locked in a rolling embrace, a sweet reassurance we would get past the fight. But something was not quite right. He didn't seem to be having fun, and gradually his enthusiasm waned.

Finally, I asked, "Is something wrong?"

"Not really," he said.

"Do you not want to be dating me?" I asked. It seemed way too bald to blurt that out, and I winced, thinking I was horribly paranoid to jump directly to break up.

He went still. After a moment said, "Well, I don't want to be *obligated*."

The way he pronounced *obligated* with a lot of emphasis on the first syllable, it might as well have been *gangrenous*.

I pushed him off of me, possibly with more force than was really needed. "Well, if you don't want to be obligated, then you shouldn't have moved in here with me."

He said nothing and pulled the sheet up over himself.

I leapt out of bed, grabbed my pillow and nightgown, and went out to the couch. As I lay down, all sorts of horrible things went through my mind. Horrible true things. Like: *You didn't even talk about it before he moved in. The two of you never agreed that you wouldn't see other people. He's been using you for a free place to stay (and sex) until his apartment is ready. And he was able to do this, because you were too timid to have a conversation about what it meant and didn't mean, and how much rent he'd pay. You allowed it. All he did was push to see what he could get away with.*

Within five minutes I knew I wouldn't be able to sleep with him on the other side of the wall, in my bed. I wanted away from him and the humiliation that he'd had to tell me mid-sex that he didn't want to be obligated. I wanted to run. I threw some clothes and my toothbrush in a backpack, found my sleeping bag, called my brother, and asked if I could come crash on his floor.

"Are you OK?" he asked.

"Yeah," I said, "but there's a jerk and a liar in my apartment, and I need to get away."

I stuck my head in the bedroom, told Blake I was going, and finished with, "Leave your key in the morning."

"Thanks for not throwing me out," he said quietly.

A wave of heat started at my face and burned over my whole body. I set the sleeping bag down.

At that moment, a psych seminar about recovery from traumatic events flashed in my mind. The main idea was that rather than repeatedly reliving a bad experience and asking why, a person can choose to believe

Obligated

she is braver, smarter, and more competent. If she does that, profound changes can occur.

My mind zipped on to how I could rewrite this story so I wouldn't roil in humiliation forever.

I needed to kick him out.

"You know," I said, "me kicking you out would be the best thing, really. I want you to leave. Now."

"But where am I gonna go? My house won't be ready for five more weeks. You're a social worker; you're supposed to care about housing for people, aren't you?"

Although I've never hit anyone, the urge to slap the hell out of his face shot through me. I clenched my hands at my sides. "You're a Republican; you're supposed to be disgusted with free-loaders who don't provide their own housing, aren't you? Maybe you should call Rosemary."

"It's 2 a.m.," he said, "and Rosemary is staying with friends."

"Ah," I said, "much as you are. Or were. Well, I don't know where you're going to go, but you're not staying here."

"I'm not gonna call and wake them up," he said.

"How thoughtful. Get your stuff out of my storage unit, too."

He tipped his head and opened his eyes wide. "Tonight? Where am I going to put all that stuff?"

"Put it in your car."

"Can't I get the stuff in the storage unit later?"

"Yeah, OK," I said. The suitcases in my storage unit would not prevent me from sleeping. "But that stuff has to be gone next week or I'm throwing it out."

"Can I sleep in the storage unit with my stuff tonight?"

"Sure," I said. "I've done it when I bombed for fleas. It's not bad. I'll even give you a blanket. You just have to get out of here." The flea bomb thing was a lie. I'd never even thought about sleeping in that hellhole, but at that point, I'd have said anything to make him leave.

"What about a pillow?"

"Nope, it's too dirty in there. Use a suitcase for a pillow. Now go. I've got to work in the morning."

I threw the scratchiest wool blanket I had at him. "I'll unlock the storage unit for you, but you've got to be gone tomorrow by ten, and I need your key."

He shrugged on his jacket and backpack, took the key off his keychain, and slapped it on the kitchen counter.

The storage unit—a plywood closet with a cement floor in a row of similar units—stood about fifty feet outside my apartment. I removed the lock and opened the flimsy door. Suitcases, boxes, a lawn chair, a cooler, and a garden hose lay crammed in a heap. "With a little creativity, I'm sure you can make it work."

I went back in my apartment, locked the door, called my brother, and told him to forget it, I was fine.

"How many people are in your apartment?" he asked.

"Just me."

"So are you the jerk or the liar?"

"The liar," I said. "Anyway, sorry I woke you up."

I couldn't bring myself to get in the bed. It seemed obscene the things we'd been doing there not even an hour ago, before he'd told me he didn't want to be obligated. So I settled on the couch.

I knew this was better, kicking him out, rather than slinking away myself, but still I felt horrid, like an unpaid prostitute, like yesterday's trash set out by the curb. "Be kind," I said to myself, in the voice I would use with a client.

I managed to wrangle my self-disgust down to feeling clumsy and clueless, kind of like a kindergartner wearing one oven mitt and one boxing glove, trying to build a snow fort. I was never telling anybody about this—not my sister, the Queen of Marriage, and not Alan, the prescient condemner, nobody.

The next morning, I bolted my breakfast, desperate to get away before he woke up. I didn't want to see his face, see myself through his eyes. I crept outside. The door to the storage unit hung open. Blake sprawled across boxes, his feet on a suitcase, his head resting on the coiled garden hose. He snored with his mouth agape.

I gently pushed the door closed, and wedged a stick through the metal loop where the lock goes to hold it shut. I walked to my car without a sound.

I knew it was likely that upon waking he would think he'd been locked in, and kick the door down. I knew this would cost me a lot of money I didn't have.

"I'll pay," I said. "However much it costs, it's still a better deal than living with him." A smile spread across my face as I started the car.

THE ADJUNCT

Allison
Age: 40
February 2006

THE ADJUNCT

"Shut your eyes." Billy pulled a crumpled paper bag from his back pocket.

I closed my eyes, and he placed something cold, metal, and angular in my palm.

"Can I look now?"

"Yes!"

It was a shiny gold pin, shaped like a cursive letter A.

"A for Allison," he said. "Do you like it?"

"I love it! Thank you, it's beautiful. Why don't you pin it on my lapel?"

While he fumbled with the catch, I pushed my chest against his hands, trying to distract him.

We were in the apartment he shared with his girlfriend, just the two of us, playing "Lara Croft, Tomb Raider," and he let me win. I cheered and bounced on the couch. It was so sweet he'd picked that game. He knew I would like it because it had a female protagonist.

The Adjunct

I'd worn the fitted black suit, my hair in a French twist, and the red heels to make him want me more. I had a class to teach in a few hours, where most of my colleagues would have on khakis, and nobody but me would look like an attorney trying to seduce the D.A., but Billy didn't know that. I told him, "Yeah, work clothes. At the university, we have to dress up, and today there's a meeting for the adjunct Profs."

"You've got the junk, all right!" he put his hands on either side of my waist.

"Adjunct. It means supplementary, extra, not the real thing. No security, no benefits."

"I've got some benefits for you," he said, stepping back. He ran his hand over the pin and around the curve of my breast. "That looks so fine. It's like that story we read in class, with the chick who had to wear the red 'A,'" he said. "Heather somebody."

"Hester, Hester Prynne. Good for you! I bet you're the only one of my students who remembers *The Scarlet Letter*."

Was he calling me an adulteress? The thought flitted through my mind. Nah. He wasn't that deep.

He probably *was* the only one who remembered—the only one from the community college where I had taught American literature to students on their way to tech degrees. My class fulfilled the English requirement, and interested no one. The day we met, Billy, at least ten years my junior, had swaggered into my class all tough-looking, on the prowl, like one of the Jets in *West Side Story*. He'd given me smoldering looks from the first time I called the roll. Of course we waited to hook up until the grades were in. I had principles.

We had dated for several years, but it was never a stable thing. When we were together, he was fiery, self-absorbed, and unstable. Much of the time I wanted out. But after we'd split, I remembered the good and forgot all the very valid reasons I left.

I looked down at the pin. "I'm wearing this because it's my initial, and it's beautiful, not because I've done anything wrong."

"Aw, you're no fun," he said. "C'mon, let's do something wrong."

I didn't think of myself as the other woman. Rather, I saw his girlfriend, Hannah, as a vulture who had swooped in and thrown herself at him as our relationship was unraveling. If she'd been willing to wait until he was actually single, then she wouldn't be in the position of living with a man who cheated on her with his ex, in her very apartment, while she was at work.

After we broke up, he called occasionally to chat. Within a few months, he asked if I would consider meeting him at a hotel, and I said no. I was shocked he would cheat on her because he was the devoted, obsessed sort.

The Adjunct

When we were dating, he made it seem like I was his whole world. I told him I was disappointed he would be that kind of person, and he said he wouldn't cheat—except he missed me so much.

So our secret meetings began. He didn't have much to say except he missed me. He'd give me one of his looks and kiss me, and my will to resist had dissolved.

He said Hannah made him feel needed and wanted, and even though sex with me was way hotter, he couldn't let her go. He was so much nicer to me during our affair than when we were a couple, and couldn't have been a better lover. After lunch and sex, we would play video games—seemed so normal at the time.

Then from out of nowhere, he said, "I have an idea—why don't you shit on me in the bathtub?"

"What? Why?"

"It'll be so hot."

He was adventurous, but meticulously clean, and I wondered if he understood what a mess and smell it would be.

He took my hand, leaned in and kissed me. A soft, melting kiss.

"How would that be a turn on?" I asked.

"Just so…uh, so hot. C'mon," he said, "let's do it in the bathtub."

"In the tub?" I asked, swinging the red stiletto from my toes.

He looked at the shoe and touched it lightly. "Yeah. Keep it contained and all. I want to experience every part of you." He brushed back a curl that had escaped my French twist.

After the initial shock settled, a surge of warmth flared through my chest, and my face got hot. I got the sense deep in my gut that ours was a deeply soulful connection, deeper than anything most people ever experience.

He wanted all of me—even the dirty aspects, no part unacceptable. As Walt Whitman said, "Welcome is every organ and attribute of me,...Not an inch nor a particle of an inch is vile, and none shall be less familiar than the rest."

For the first time ever, maybe, I was being fully seen and valued. I felt so much desire for him. I can honestly say, I've never wanted a man more.

I looked around. Empty soda cans littered the coffee table, which was piled with *People* magazines. Mugs with scum in the bottom sat on every flat surface. A pile of newspapers on the floor at the end of the couch was almost tall enough to serve as an end table.

Wow, I thought, all this could have been mine. I could have had this—with him. The kitchen table, heaped with junk mail and over-ripe bananas with a few fruit flies circling, had one leg propped on a piece of folded cardboard. A happy-face mug with a dark lipstick stain sat in front of a chair where Hannah probably had her breakfast. Old bacon grease hovered in the air.

I leaned back against the couch. With each minute that slid by, the thought of the bathtub thing became more disconcerting.

Although just about every time with him was great, I didn't want to be covered in shit. Once, he'd tied me to their bed with silk scarves, and the sex had been mind blowing. But this? I wasn't so sure.

"Um, well, I don't have to go," I said.

He lifted my chin gently with one hand and caressed the side of my face with the other. His eyes were the most tender and romantic I'd ever seen them. "That's OK," he said, "I'll give you an enema."

It was hard to believe he'd just made that suggestion, although I was touched that he was enthusiastic about giving me an enema. It seemed nurturing and caretaking. Since there is no one on earth I would look forward to giving an enema to, it made me feel oddly special.

"But I'm all ready for work, and I don't—what if Hannah comes home?"

I looked over at the dishes piled in the sink—they were feuding over who should do them. Apparently they had a deal: since she was only working part time, she was to take care of the apartment, but didn't. He said she was "lazy, crazy, and never kept her word."

I began to wonder if he felt a need to be punished or humiliated for leaving me, especially for a woman he didn't seem to like or respect. I hoped he felt he should be punished anyway.

It dawned on me slowly; *she* is the one he loves. And no, they don't really connect on a sexual level, yet he loves her. Me, he fucks. And wants to punish himself with dirty, filthy me, defecating on him, because he is cheating on the woman he loves. That thought and the "A" gleaming on my lapel gave me a terrible ache in my gut, and sweat broke out on my forehead.

Yes, he did deserve to be punished, and hell yeah, I might as well be the one to administer it. I imagined making a giant mess on him in the tub, and getting some on the floor and the bathmat. Then I could abruptly leave him there like that. Just like that.

Just as suddenly, I began to despise myself. I wrenched my butt off the sagging couch.

"Think how terrible it would be if Hannah comes home while we're in the tub—as crazy jealous as she is, and how would you get everything cleaned up?" I asked.

He shrugged and took his feet off the coffee table. Was he looking for an easy way to get rid of her? Maybe he really wanted me.

He stroked my leg, and I snapped back to the moment of decision.

I stood in front of him, slowly turned my back, and said over my shoulder, "Are the seams up the backs of my stockings straight?"

It gave me a few moments, while he knelt and ran his mouth and nose up and down those seams. A thrill, small but discernible, rippled through me, although I felt about six thousand miles away. My head whirled.

Finally, the reasoning part of my brain engaged. This is not about him loving and accepting me deeply, and it is not about him loving her and wanting to punish himself for cheating. What an immense relief, and the leading edge of a wave of shock. This is not about me or her. It's about him wanting a kink. It's just him wanting to get off, and needing greater and greater debauchery to do so. It is all about him. It's always been only about him. A massive door started creaking shut inside me, a door with rust-encrusted hinges.

"What time is it?" I looked down at him crouched on the rug, trying to push his head under the back of my skirt.

He pulled back and looked at his watch.

I grabbed his arm. "Whoa! I'm going to be late if I don't scoot. I've got that meeting today before class." I pulled him to his feet and watched the disappointment wash over his face. He put a hand on my butt.

In the Glow of the Lavalamp

"Sorry, babe, I lost track of time there. Interesting idea about the tub, but right now I've got to run."

I kissed him, reapplied my lipstick carefully, and cleaned up the smudges at the corners of my eyeliner, as if putting the finishing touches on stage makeup. He watched me hungrily.

"So maybe next time?" he said, squeezing my butt with both hands.

"I guess nothing is completely impossible." I adjusted my cleavage.

"I'll walk you out."

"Probably better not," I said. "Sounds like lots of people downstairs in the lobby. You never know who might see us, and I don't want to get you in trouble."

He kissed the "A," his breath fogging the metal, kissed the bridge of my nose, and finally my mouth.

I gave him a quick peck, grabbed my purse, and slipped out the door, closing it silently behind me, as if slipping away from a crime scene.

My shoes clipped the stairs like hooves, and I felt about as steady as a pig on linoleum. I had the pin unhooked by the time I hit the street.

In the car, I wiped off the red lipstick and threw the cursive A on the floor. My notes for class waited on the seat like some kind of church lady reminding me that I had responsibilities in the real world, classes to teach, colleagues, friends—solid stuff that didn't have to be hidden.

Out on the highway, my head cleared some more. I drove five miles or so, pulled onto the shoulder and got out, the wind biting at my face. Cold and bracing air blasted away the lingering whiffs of him. When my hands went numb, I climbed into the passenger side and held my stacks of papers for class. I hugged them to my chest like a sacred document. I paged through the notes—Emily Dickinson. Maybe this was a sign I'd be a spinster, isolated forever. Maybe I needed to retreat or move to New England. Why did everything have to mean something? I was tired of symbolism and trying to make sense of stuff that made no sense.

I flipped to the end of the lecture notes.

"Oh Emily, help me," I said.

And then I found it, Dickinson's poem about letting go. What did Emily Dickinson know about letting go? Probably more than I did. Hell, an anal-retentive two-year-old knew more than I did about letting go.

I read the last of it aloud.

> *This is the Hour of Lead –*
> *Remembered, if outlived,*
> *As Freezing persons, recollect the Snow –*
> *First – Chill – then Stupor – then the letting go –*

In the Glow of the Lavalamp

I climbed out of the car, clutching the metal A, and looked at the distorted slice of my face reflected in it. I threw it hard, overhand, into the culvert.

PART TWO
Other Misfortunes

THE SAMPLE

"No urine!" the lab tech warned me. "No water from the toilet. Do you understand, Ms. Williams?"

Yes, I did understand. The tech had called to give me instructions to produce a fecal sample at home; supposedly with more privacy and less rush, I'd be more relaxed.

You'd think.

She told me they usually gave people containers but I could bring mine in a Tupperware.

I gathered up paper plates, Popsicle sticks, hiking boots, Tupperware, a radio, and the phone, and headed into my tiny, relaxing bathroom. My "Tupperware" was a plastic container with a lid labeled "Hummus, Original Flavor." The phone was in case my boss or my mother called, so I could be reassuringly normal. I was also fielding calls from the realtor, the mortgage broker, and the flooring guy about things that had seemed

The Sample

urgent just days ago. Certainly, trying to combine any of these calls with the present endeavor was not a good idea. But I had left the land of common sense far behind and was now solidly in the realm of crisis, where people do things like clutching a cell phone while trying to produce a stool sample.

The phone was a reminder that my life was busy and moving forward; I'd made an offer on a house. The health concerns were minor, not catastrophic.

So to the task I turned, charged with enough adrenaline to lift a hippo. It's not like I'm phobic about my own body waste—I mean, hell, it's simply the food you've eaten, the part your body no longer needs, being discarded, nothing to freak out over. Still, I'd never handled it before, and being scared made the task more difficult.

I'd heard about fecal occult blood testing. Yes, I knew it meant hidden blood, but occult? So were they testing for channeling ability? Ghosts? I'd seen the kits; the corporation I worked for provided them to us every five years as a health initiative. And we, the arrogantly healthy, had used them for office jokes. Each kit had a wooden stick, and a small, very small card upon which a smear was placed for a microscope slide. Only the tiniest amount was required. I mean, some people who forget to wash their hands probably carry more to the dinner table. So I was going for a very modest-sized specimen.

The whole affair sounds simpler than it is. Once everything was arranged, my body froze and refused to cooperate, so I turned on the radio and found a station playing old Baptist hymns. "What a friend we have in Jeeeeeezus, all our sins and griefs to bear…"

The lower half my torso had turned to cement, unmoved by the church music. My lungs felt like they were shrinking. The phone rang. I jumped and threw the paper plate aside. The mortgage guy could leave a message. I put the phone in the bathtub, where it buzzed and spun in circles.

I kept on singing. "Have we trials and temptations? Is there trouble anywhere?"

Many paper plates and half a roll of toilet paper later, I achieved the desired result. In the excitement of victory, I made a jerky grab for the Tupperware, knocking the radio into the trash and my brand new $75 skin-cancer lotion off the sink. It vaulted through the air in slow motion, flipping end over end, the top ricocheting off the shower wall, and the tube itself lighting squarely on top of the sample, as if pulled by a homing device.

At this point, I was yelling the hymn with a strong emphasis on the "cumbered with a load of care" and a few other words. It would've been easier and far less of a mess if I'd just yanked my pants off and aimed for the

The Sample

floor. Eventually, I got the mission accomplished (no water, no urine, no skin cancer lotion) and corralled the specimen into the Tupperware. I snapped the lid on and put it in the fridge. As I put all the stuff away, I wondered what normal people across the nation were doing. Teaching arithmetic, cutting the grass, writing memos. I wanted their ordinary lives.

Hours later I arrived at the lab with the Tupperware in a tasteful brown bag. With my gut gnawing and jaw clenched, I tiptoed into the giant waiting room. Lots of weary-looking people sat in a syrup of resignation. Resignation to endless waiting, claim forms, lab tests, and less-than-hopeful treatments with horrible side effects. Probably a lot of them were waiting to hear if their liver was still intact or the cancer had completely destroyed their two remaining blood cells.

Mine's not that serious, I told myself.

I left my name at the desk and sat down by a woman with a large hot pink shell glued on her hair clip. It looked like something from a souvenir shop at the beach. She held a worn McDonald's Fillet-of-Fish box, rubber-banded together. With my eyes averted, my brain circled the box. *I bet that's not your lunch*, I thought. A small boy seated beside her was engrossed in his book.

Looking around at the other patients and pondering whether it was the boy or his grandmother who was seriously ill was not doing me any good, so I dredged up all the New Agey-ness I could remember and began to concentrate on wellness and healing white light. Shortly the white light was beaming down on a vision of me opened up on the operating table having a bowel resection. I don't know exactly what a bowel resection is, or what illness it treats, but it's pretty serious. The doors of the future were slamming rapidly. Sex, dancing, swimming, wearing normal clothes, and even laughing hard were looking like things of the past. Why was I buying a house?

The fish fillet lady put her hand on my knee and said, "Don't do that, darlin'."

I jumped. "What?" Her hand was warm and comforting. "Sorry, you startled me. Don't do what?"

She smiled. "See if you can get your shoulders off your ears, honey."

I slowly let my shoulders down. "Good idea," I said, giving her a little smile. I sat there, feeling myself untwist just the tiniest bit, and wished I never had to get out of the chair.

After a while, a woman in scrubs called me back through the swinging doors, and I went, clutching the paper bag. She grinned and said, "Come right on back here, baby girl."

Looking like a Dr. Seuss character in her purple latex gloves, she studied my paperwork.

I held the bag out to her. "I brought a sample."

All the techs in the area turned with big saucer eyes, so I took the hummus container out. "It's clean," I said. "I mean it was a clean container to begin with."

They stared.

What? It's not like I was holding a two-pounder in my bare hands.

Baby Girl Tech gave me a pair of beautiful purple gloves, just like hers, and I put them on, like a happy cartoon character. Still she did not take the sample from me. Instead, she gathered up a fistful of vials and motioned me to follow her into a restroom.

"I would do this for you," she said, grimacing, "but I'd get sick. It's better if you do it; normally the patient has the kit at home."

"I understand," I said, feeling like a vulgar, red-faced peasant who had just asked her to do something unspeakable. A mist of sweat popped out on my forehead. A lab tech squeamish about body waste? Maybe she wasn't a real tech, just administrative. Maybe this was managed care—having the patients process their own lab tests. Maybe I was uncouth.

She opened a bottle and showed me a tiny spoon attached to the lid. "Use this," she said, "to scoop a little bit of it into each vial. Then screw the tops on. Each one has a different fluid in it for a different test. Then with the bigger one, use this wooden stick to put in enough to bring the liquid up to the red line. It has to reach the red line, see?"

"Yes," I said, swallowing hard, "I get it. I hope I have enough." Where was the card? I thought this test was just putting a little smear on a card.

"Well, try really hard to bring it up to the red line," she said, pointing. "It really needs to come up to the red line."

I glared at the vials. How was I supposed to try really hard? She left, and I locked the door and sat on the floor with all the stuff. Four vials. Reaching the red line. The inadequate taking-a-math-test feeling set in. But I had come this far and would make a go of it.

I peeled back the lid on the Tupperware and started scooping with the tiny spoons. I was dismayed to find that poop displaces very little water. So little, in fact, that this was probably worthy of scientific investigation. By somebody else.

I fixed the first three, with the tiny spoons, then turned to the big one. The one where I had to bring the fluid up to the red line. My sample was almost gone. I scraped and dug with the little wooden stick.

I thought maybe if I flung it into the vial with great force it would displace more of the liquid, bringing it closer to the red line, which now seemed far away. I wasn't sure about the physics, but it seemed worth trying, otherwise I wouldn't be able to pass the test. It's hard to fling poop with any precision. It made a little sound like *thpikk* when it hit the tile wall, and looked like an innocent mud splatter. The little wooden stick worked equally well for scraping the sample off the wall as it did from the Tupperware.

It quickly became apparent that I was not going to be anywhere in the vicinity of the red line; neither mass, nor velocity, nor force was going do it. Cursing the loss of all the good stuff I'd carelessly flushed away, I peered into the now empty hummus container. How could I have been so stupid—assuming we were dealing with the occult? I considered a dash to the waiting room to see if the fish fillet lady would spare me some of her sample. I knew she would help me if she could. Or maybe I could put in a wad of chewing gum. I stared at my shoes, wishing they had mud, or even dog poop on them, so I could put that in the vial.

Finally I gave up, cleaned the wall, and took the vials out to the tech.

"It's all I have," I said, fighting tears. "I don't have enough to do them all."

"Baby, that's OK," she said. "You can bring some more later."

I nodded, and pushed through the swinging doors into the overwhelm, all around me now like a bank of fog.

In the waiting room, the lady with the pink shell was gone. The young boy sat alone squeezing a peanut butter and jelly sandwich and studying the cross-section after each bite. The open Fillet-of-Fish container was on his lap.

He grinned and held the sandwich up so I could see the strata in it. "Look at the layers!" he said. "Looks like a mountain, and then there's a valley."

"That's great!" I said, staring. I flashed back on driving home from college at Thanksgiving, junior year, snow flying, the miles whizzing by. Suddenly my VW Bug slid, bounced hard in the median, and careened to the other side of the interstate, slicing diagonally across the lanes and missing an eighteen-wheeler by inches. My car finally came to a stop on the shoulder, headed the wrong way—my own sandwich on the edge of the dash squarely in front of me. I had stared at the peanut butter and jelly, confirming I was alive, and erupted tears. The sandwich symbolized something, I was sure—another chance to live, to try again. Over time, I had forgotten it. And now, here this child smiling at his own sandwich, seeing landscapes and who knows what else, elbowed me off the path of panic and despair.

"Thanks for showing me," I said. "I'm going to get a sandwich like that."

THE CHRISTMAS TREE

December had settled in over east Tennessee like a well-chilled shroud, and I was sure that getting a Christmas tree would make life better. Three years of archaeology grad school had frayed my soul—too much time living off ramen noodles and digging up plastic streamers from bicycle handlebars rather than finding the eighteenth-century trash pit I sought. I was desperate to have a little sweetness in my life.

In my large family, we drew names, so I had to purchase just one gift. I'd pinched more pennies than usual to buy my niece an illustrated copy of Hans Christian Andersen's *Fairy Tales*, complete with the "The Emperor's New Clothes," "The Ugly Duckling," and the morbid tale of "The Little Match Girl." This little match girl was a poverty-stricken child who spent her days selling matches alone in the filth and bustle of the city streets while holiday shoppers brushed past. Freezing and

The Christmas Tree

hungry, she decided to light the matches one by one, to savor the warmth and light for the short time they burned. Finally, she set a whole bundle ablaze, delighted with the glorious glow. Then she froze to death.

So yeah. Uplifting.

I considered cutting those pages out of the book. The story was way too depressing. Or maybe I was just depressed. I let it be and wrapped the present.

Now it was time for my gift. The tree. I saw myself lying on the floor, staring up through the pine-scented branches and the twinkling lights.

I wanted that tree and I knew just where to get it. A rock quarry backed up to the property where I was doing archaeological work for my thesis, and in that quarry was a wonderland of young cedars.

One chilly afternoon when we finished digging, I convinced my friend Rick to help me cut a tree. We had a hacksaw with a blade as sharp as a butter knife. Right in front of us, just across the property line, stood a cedar, about my height, and sort of symmetrical, if you closed one eye. By tackling the tree and bending it till it almost snapped, we managed to gnaw it down with the old saw.

My face dripped with sweat and guilt for making him work so hard, and I asked, "Don't you want one too?"

He laughed and said, "Why not?"

In the Glow of the Lavalamp

We edged further into the quarry, our breath making frosty clouds in the air. The second tree took slightly less effort, but it was still unbelievably difficult, so I must've been either short of oxygen or filled with the holiday spirit when I suggested we cut a third tree for his girlfriend, Deb, who'd been depressed lately.

"It'll cheer her up," I said.

He raised his eyebrows. "You sure?"

"I know it!" I said, with the bold vigor of one who sees what is best for everybody.

In the belly of the quarry, a six-foot, round-looking cedar beckoned. Huffing and sweating in our jackets, we sawed it down and dragged all three to the car, a little Dodge Colt.

We wedged the first two into the trunk. They both stuck out, and we tied the lid halfway down to hold them. We put the big one on the roof, tying it to the front and back bumpers, and looping the twine sideways through the windows, effectively tying the doors shut. We would have to climb in the windows to go home. The car looked so festive loaded with evergreens—we were clapping when the police pulled up.

Rick and I looked at each other wide-eyed and both uttered a single word, which roughly translates as, *Oh dear. This doesn't seem to be going well.*

The Christmas Tree

I've heard that dying people have their lives flash before them, but at that moment, only the grad school part of mine flashed. The papers, tests, student loans, hours in the lab, days in the field digging, everything flew by me. I saw it all circling the drain, and my career going to the sewer before it started.

Tomorrow the news would read: "Grad student arrested for stealing Christmas trees. Ms. Wilson, doing research on the property adjacent to the quarry, has been expelled from the university." Everything inside me collapsed, like shuffled, feathered, playing cards.

I saw myself in jail, no one to call. I saw my naïve attachment to a pagan Christmas tradition as foolish. I hated myself for taking something that wasn't mine (three of them!), for making my friend accessory to theft, and for giving up my future for an emotional indulgence.

All this swept by in less than a minute. The police came farther up the drive behind my car, which looked like a huge lumpy evergreen shrub with wheels. Rick and I both raised a hand to wave, showing we were harmless. I was holding the hack saw, so I waved with it.

The cops waved back, one holding a cup of coffee. A box of Krispy Kremes rested on their dash. They put the car in reverse and backed out, went on down the road.

Rick snorted. "Looks like they're working on an important case."

I did not laugh; I was still dealing with a serious heart arrhythmia and trying to decide if I should toss the hacksaw into the quarry.

"Gimme the keys," said Rick.

We climbed in the windows and he started the car, chuckling, "Donuts!"

Loaded with three Christmas trees and a pile of archaeological equipment, we looked like a Far Side cartoon as we crept down the road away from the donut eaters. Rick made his way to the interstate carefully, mindful of our cargo, now even more precious after a glimpse of what the cost might have been. I helped by holding my weight off the seat with one hand.

On the highway, we both breathed easier. At this point, we were just people with cedars. We saw others with trees, but most of them had only one. I waved at everybody; it was fun being a Christmas-tree-toting American. We laughed about how scary it had been, and were saying "I thought for sure we were dead, and I thought…" when the tree on top of the car started to slip.

I grabbed the twine at the window, and it came loose in my hand. The tree took flight off the roof like a missile. We both yelled, and my insides dropped as I imagined the tree going through the windshield of the car

The Christmas Tree

behind us, butt end first, at sixty miles per hour, impaling the driver in the face.

I twisted in my seat, but with the trunk tied part way up over the two trees, I couldn't see what was happening.

Once more, my life flashed away. This time I was in jail for manslaughter, and the family of the deceased had sued me, and I had $13.00 in my checking account. How terrible to have killed someone in such a gruesome and festive way. The newspaper articles were about the same as I'd thought of before, except now they included stuff about the death, and speculation on whether we had intended to sell the trees.

Rick said, "We'd better pull over."

"Yeah," I said. "We better."

He edged onto the shoulder and so did the vehicle behind us. We climbed out the windows, now loosely wreathed in twine.

I was stunned with relief to see the unbroken windshield on the van parked behind us. The tree was halfway in a ditch, squashed. I gulped, followed Rick toward the driver's side, and scanned the van for damage.

As we got close, the guy put his window down, and big clouds of marijuana smoke billowed out, surrounding us in a giant puff.

The driver, young, with a scraggly beard and a plaid jacket, stuck his head out and blurted, "Oh *man*! We ran over your

Christmas tree! Man, I'm sorry! We didn't mean to do that! *Man!* This is terrible."

His friend in a hunting hat said, "Dang, man."

I stood blinking in the smoke, unable to speak.

"Look," Rick said harshly, leaning toward the guy, "from now on be more careful. And just don't ever do it again!"

He turned abruptly, threw me a sharp elbow, and we marched back to the Colt with indignation, leaving the tree without a glance.

Snapping out his pocketknife, Rick cut the twine so we could open the doors and get in the car with some dignity.

"Those guys," I said, feeling my life coming back, "those guys were really stoned."

"Ya think?" He merged into traffic.

In my side mirror I saw the guy with the hunting hat get out of the van. Maybe he was taking a whiz, maybe he was taking the tree, I didn't care. He was welcome to it.

"So," said Rick, "you gonna put up your tree tonight?"

I turned, ready to bite him, saw the earnest look on his face, and realized what a grasping idiot I'd become.

"Put up the tree?" I said. "No, I don't think so. I might set it on fire, for the spectacle and all, you know? Like the Little Match Girl."

Big Luck

BIG LUCK

Most of us learned in elementary school that George Washington had false teeth made of wood, but this is not true. He had a number of sets of dentures over the years, but they were made of teeth from pigs, cows, and humans, as well as rhino horns mounted on lead plates and hinged with little springs in the back. The man had terrible teeth and spent a lot of time in pain as they rotted and abscessed.

I was recovering from an ordinary but excruciating root canal and feeling some kinship with old George as I made my quarterly pilgrimage to Big Lucky's, the store where the clientele is dodgy and the very best price can be had for steel-cut oats and many other things less desirable. I kept telling myself I was fortunate to live in the age of modern dentistry, but the sensation of a red-hot screw being threaded into my jaw reduced my feeling of good fortune.

"George had it worse," I muttered.

Truly he did. By the time he was president, he had only one of his own teeth still in his head. And even once he got the replacements, it wasn't over. His letters indicate that the fakes were too big and hurt his gums. In his portraits, you can see his cheeks puffed out to accommodate the too-wide dentures. For dental pain, he took laudanum, an opiate derivative popular in the eighteenth century.

So he was dealing with the ongoing pain, the ill-fitting choppers, and narcotic haze, all that, as he led the weary troops to victory, helped hammer out the bones of our government, and served as president. He was a tough guy. A lesser man might've simply become a drunk and nursed his pain in the gutter.

I found the steel-cut oats and took a lap around the store, trying to distract myself from the giant set of pliers squeezing the bone in the area of my molars.

Right beside the Wonder Woman lunch boxes were some with George Washington on the front. I was studying the lunch boxes when something unexpected and distinctly wet slid into my pants. My brain instantly denied it had happened. Nope, not me. Sometimes, after a week or so, antibiotics will wreak havoc with your gut. But this was day two of a round that went with the root canal. No warning stomach cramps, no signal it was about to happen, nothing.

I'm guessing this is what children and naïve men think giving birth is like. Something slips out of your body, causing no pain, in fact being something of a surprise, since there was absolutely no indication it was imminent. Except in those cases, everybody is delighted with the new arrival.

My denial crumbled like GW's lousy teeth, and there was a distinct absence of delight about the thing that had just happened to me.

I assumed that Big Lucky's had no bathroom. This was for the best, because if it did, that bathroom would be the kind of place where a madwoman pushes your face down on the baby-changing shelf and cuts out one of your kidneys with a pocketknife. I told myself that I could go to the nice clean ladies' room at the grocery across the street and take care of the mess, only a small problem. I moved toward the checkout, with not one thought of purchasing something useful like the jumbo pack of paper towels, a muumuu to wear home, or a box of Depends. Nope, I was buying my three-month supply of steel-cut oats, as if the future of civilization depended on it.

The checkout line was mercifully short, but the guy in front of me was chatting with the cashier about his key chain. His key chain! I bumped his cart gently with mine, wafting a few toxic fumes his way. He gave me the fish eye but moved on. The cashier wanted to see my Big Lucky's Value Card, and if not that, enter my phone number in the database. He wanted to tell me about the specials. I wanted to get to my car unhumiliated, and without giving birth to a sibling turd.

The wetness was slowly spreading across my butt, sliding slightly to the side. Sadly, I had begun the day with rather insubstantial underwear, so this unwelcome presence was being smeared all over the inside of my khaki pants. Why had I not selected black for this occasion? Or better still, a long full skirt like those sister wives wear in religious cults?

Ever so slowly, I walked to the parking lot, like a bridesmaid with severe arthritis coming down the aisle. I wondered if a giant greasy stain was manifesting on my backside, announcing to the world the miracle that had occurred in my khakis.

My thoughts turned again to George Washington and the famous painting of him crossing the Delaware River. In this picture, Washington and eleven other people are aboard a small boat, surrounded by icebergs bobbing in the water. In a heroic but foolhardy posture, Washington is standing up in the little rowboat, at risk of capsizing the whole damn thing—no doubt to inspire the others, who are sporting their native costumes like the contestants at a Miss Universe pageant and frantically shoving away icebergs with their oars and feet. This painting has everything—height, depth, action, a broad sweeping panorama, and a giant, historically inaccurate flag furled in the wind. I now feared that it had been reproduced on the seat of my pants in all its sprawling glory.

I pressed on toward my car, parked far away, because people in the Big Lots parking lot can be kind of rough. I didn't want them near my car, selling illegal services and partaking of intoxicating substances. At that moment, however, it occurred to me that though some there may have been selling meth or hustling people, everyone I saw appeared to have managed to do their business in a bathroom.

I could feel the mass shifting in my pants. It was beginning to dawn on me that this situation might be too big for the ladies' room at the grocery. My house was six miles away, but it might as well have been sixty. I made my steps smaller and smaller, but like George Washington, held my head aloft, intent upon my goal.

And then some guy yelled, "Excuse me! Miss!"

I turned with a daggery look. Surely he wasn't going to notify me that I had a mess on my rear end. If he dared to point out reality, I was going to beat him to death with my steel-cut oats.

He stared my way, glassy eyed, waved a bottle of Windex, and said, "Help you clean up?"

"What?" I snapped. What exactly was he offering to clean?

"Your windshield. Clean your windshield?"

I shook my head, mumbled, "No thanks," and turned sideways as I continued on, so he couldn't see the back of me.

As I crept along, I dug in my purse for the keys and found none. Maybe I'd dropped them in the store and would now have to re-cross the parking lot, evade the Windex guy again, go back inside, and bend over to grab the keys off the floor.

Just as I reached the car, a bit of material broke loose from the main mass and began a descent down the leg of my pants. I stood staring into space as the breakaway blob grazed my knee and made a silent landing on the pavement beside my shoe. It was about the size of a quarter, the consistency of something between applesauce and wet cement, and could have been the head of president-to-be James Monroe, who crouches beside Washington in the painting, holding the flag aloft. This was one less bit I was carrying now. I was glad as well as horrified. I stood searching for the keys, and hoped the rest of the scene would also exit my pant leg, and I could go home as if nothing had happened.

Well, of course things weren't going to go that way, but I was still glad to be rid of Monroe's head. I started back toward the store, cursing quietly, like a crazy person. Washington and his soldiers truly had it rough, but once they crossed the river and landed in New Jersey, they didn't have to turn around and go back for somebody's keys.

When I reached the store, I slipped my sandals off and left them under the Big Lucky's sign in the front window. If I could pick up the keys with my toes, I wouldn't have to bend over and make the problem worse.

I threw back my shoulders and marched in with a military bearing and a big smile. "Hey there!" I said to the guy behind the counter. "I think I dropped my keys here." I walked sideways toward the lunchbox aisle, grinning at him.

"You can't come in here barefoot," he said. "You got to have shoes."

"I've got shoes," I said. "They're in the car, and I need my keys."

He stepped out from behind the counter. "You must leave *now*," he said. "No shoes, no service."

The poor man didn't realize I could befoul half the store before he got back behind the safety of the counter.

"OK," I said. "I'm buying flip flops, and I'll put them right on and pay for them. Where are the flip flops?"

He pointed to the door. "I'm sorry ma'am, you have to leave now, or I'm going to call the manager."

"Go ahead," I said. "I'll just grab my keys."

The keys were not with the lunchboxes or the steel-cut oats, and he was closing in on me.

I backed away. "I was wrong, no keys here. Thanks for letting me look," I said, fleeing to the door. I put on my shoes and hurried across the parking lot, expecting the manager to come running after me. I did not care how big a mess I made or who saw it.

I dumped the purse out on the hood of the car. The keys had been in the bottom all along.

I put a shopping bag on the driver's seat and slowly sat down. This was rather unpleasant, but probably nothing compared to what the passengers in Washington's boat suffered, seated in icy water, in a blinding storm, with their leader in a valiant but precarious pose, showing off his watch fob and tipping the boat. Maybe he was buzzed on Laudanum. Still, strutting the watch fob at a time of war crisis?

In the painting, the watch fob dangling near his crotch supposedly looks so much like the rounded end of an anatomical part that censorship has at times been thought necessary. As recently as 1999, the distressed Muscogee County, Georgia, Board of Education had the teacher's aides hand paint out the timepiece in thousands of history textbooks that carried scandalous uncensored copies of the painting.

I had no watch fob. My shame was nowhere near that big, although my challenge felt equally daunting. As I drove home, jaw throbbing, I considered the frozen food with me—stuff I'd purchased in my life BBL, Before Big Lucky's. I was a different person now, a person who needed a strategy. I came up with this: let that frozen stuff melt while I change clothes.

My voyage was done. I had persevered like Washington and his troops. Unlike them, I didn't have to march ten miles in the snow with bloody rags tied around my feet and attack sleeping soldiers. My khakis would never be reproduced on the New Jersey state quarter like their crossing of the Delaware. That was fine with me.

There are many things we can learn from Washington: courage, endurance, leadership—just about everything but boat safety. The lesson most pertinent for me at that moment, though, was that there's a time for relief of misery and the welcome of oblivion. I was ready for some Laudanum.

THE FUNERAL WEEKEND

We gathered boxes and went to pack up my father's apartment. It was early December, the part when everything is ramping up and the holiday mania swells. Colored lights outlined his building, glowing in the winter sun of late afternoon. Carols played in the lobby, and poinsettias were grouped around the piano. I was unsure how long my holding-it-together face would last, and I didn't want to hear condolences from strangers, so we swept through like we had an urgent errand.

My boyfriend, Bruce unlocked the door and we padded in silently. Being in Papa's apartment with him gone was like looking at a jigsaw puzzle with a piece missing. The absence of that piece delineates its own shape and the shapes of the pieces around where it should be, in sharp relief. It's like a hole blown through, and that puzzle can never be completed.

In the Glow of the Lavalamp

In the middle of the bedroom was a big stain, like coffee grounds had been spilled on the beige carpet. We ignored this and walked around it at first. We sorted books, photos, neck ties; I found the secret stash of cigarettes, found letters I'd written him; he'd saved them all. I wished I'd written him more. My heart felt tight and shrunken, as if it had gotten smaller with each letter I failed to write. On the second run for boxes, we picked up some Green Cleaner and enough paper towels to roll out a path to heaven and back.

I sprayed the hell out of the stain, which was about the size of a dinner plate. Then on hands and knees, I began to scrub it hard, my tears dripping into the mix.

Bruce came over, held out his hand for the paper towels, and asked, "You want me to do that?"

"Yes," I said, "thank you." I went into the bathroom, where my dad had actually died while getting into the shower. I cried some more, washed my face, and came back out to fold clothes and throw away the newspapers stacked by his easy chair. I stared at the dates on them and wondered what the last thing he watched on TV was.

Bruce got the rug as clean as if there never had been a mess, or a death, or any kind of stain there. This was completely unnecessary, since the condos replaced the carpet between tenants. I couldn't bear it though—none of us could bear it—looking at that stain, imagining his last hours and minutes.

We packed up the flashcards he'd been using to learn Russian, emptied the refrigerator, took the pictures off the walls, threw away medication, pipe tobacco, and his shower chair. We left the apartment spotless.

Back at my mom's place, I spoke with my sister, Rebecca, a physician, as my dad was. "I've heard of people vomiting up stuff that looks like coffee grounds," I said. "Isn't that a sign of internal bleeding? As a doctor, wouldn't Papa have known when that happened that something was bad wrong, and he needed to get help?"

"Without a doubt," she said and pressed her lips together.

"So—he knew he was possibly dying, and chose not to call for help?"

"It certainly appears that way," she said.

I felt as though the floor had collapsed under me, the wood splintering down into a bottomless dark pit. Not exactly suicide, but not that far from it, either.

I knew he'd been unhappy since he and my mother had separated, but imagining him wanting death whole-heartedly was a different thing. Guilt and sadness rolled together like a spiky briar taking up all the space under my ribs.

My sister Emily saw his wish to die not only as betrayal, but abandonment, too.

"Maybe he tried to hurry it along," she said, "popped a few ibuprofen." She dabbed at angry tears in the corners of her eyes.

My mother was instantly chin-deep in denial. "That could not possibly be. He would never have allowed it to go on," she said. "He was sick and didn't realize what was happening."

She commenced construction of an alternate story, one that replaced their fifty-year marriage, the last ten years of his life, and in particular, the twenty-four hours prior to his death with more cheerful scenarios.

I didn't contradict her—nobody did. I'd read about how people sometimes act crazy and say bizarre stuff when somebody dies.

Despite the written instructions my dad had left, requesting that my sister scatter his ashes in the flower bed at church, Mom announced that she would be taking the ashes to her home state, Indiana, for burial.

Both my parents thought divorce was wrong, and although they'd been living apart for ten years, the word "separated" was not tolerated in reference to their marriage. Mostly we didn't mention it. Mom's grim determination that Papa was going to spend eternity at her side was something of a surprise.

She asked if we, his daughters, minded. Emily rolled her eyes. Rebecca shrugged. I suggested that we put half the ashes in the flower bed at church as requested, and she could take the other half to Indiana.

She replied, "I'm going to be buried in Indiana, and he wants to be with me."

Rebecca pulled me into the kitchen and whispered, "She's going to do what she's going to do. Just get out of her way. There will be no reasoning—you will be smashed."

I knew she was right. I swallowed the outrage that bubbled up my throat, and said, "Oh. OK," though I choked on it.

Mom asked me to go buy a wreath with a white bow. She said that's what people put on the door when they're bereaved during the holidays. When Bruce and I arrived at the Christmas tree lot, business was brisk, jovial people all around us hoisting Scotch firs and spruces and calling out, "Look at this one! This one looks good."

All the wreaths sported red or metallic gold bows. I slowly unwired the red bow on one as we inched forward in the line to the cashier.

When we got to the front, I asked the guy if they could put a white bow on our wreath. "It's for a family that has had a death," I said.

The guy found a white bow, and smiling, said conversationally, "I hope it's nobody you were close to."

"My dad," I said, and a great gulping sob leapt out of me.

I shoved the wreath and money at Bruce, said I'd see him at the car, and fled through the maze of evergreens and shoppers. The cashier's apologies rang out behind me, "I'm so sorry!"

After a while Bruce showed up at the car with the wreath, white bow in place. He said the guy gave it to him free. The guy also gave him the red bow I'd removed and said it was "in case you need it later."

I took the red bow and flung it into the backseat of the car with all the luggage and stuff. It landed on the shelf under the back window and I left it there. For months.

We hung the wreath on my mom's door. Now the household was marked like the Israelites in the Bible who had to put a lamb's blood on the door to keep the angel of death away. Except it was too late for that.

***

Relatives and friends descended upon us for the funeral. As we put together a meal for the out-of-towners, my sister handed me a greyish avocado and told me to peel it for the salad. But it was way too soft to be edible, way past the guacamole stage even. The idea that anyone should be asked to endure this decaying avocado in their salad seemed monstrous. I took the squishy thing, stepped out of my mother's over-heated apartment

The Funeral Weekend

into the crisp and cloudy day, and walked to the parking lot as if I knew what I was doing.

Alongside the cars ran a narrow strip of woods, where trees and bushes had been allowed to grow as a buffer between the lot and the next property. I hurled the avocado into the woods, heaved it so hard my arm hurt. It hit a pine tree and dropped in some brambles. I exhaled a mighty sigh as if I'd fixed the giant swamp of grief and shock sucking all around me, and walked back to the apartment, relieved in a weird way.

When we put the food on the table, Rebecca kept asking, "Where's that avocado I asked you to peel?"

I acted as if I were looking for it.

Finally, she asked me so loudly that everyone paused and turned as if I were about to reveal the location of hidden treasure. I motioned her into the kitchen and told her it was too rotten and revolting and I'd thrown it into the woods. She looked surprised, stared at me with a grin, and threw her head back and burst into raucous laughter. I loved her for that. I told her it was going to make a very special holiday for some mice and a raccoon.

One of the cousins had brought along her step-daughter, Daphne, who had never even met my dad but got stuck at our funeral weekend because her own dad was on call. This poor girl, about twelve years old, one foot in adolescence and one in childhood, was truly miserable. Her bangs, in the growing-out stage, were pinned diagonally across her forehead, and spots of skin peaked through where they gapped. She was skinny, and the adults kept complimenting her on this and chuckling about their own fatness as they shoveled shortbread into their mouths. She sat tucked in a corner of the sofa with a copy of *Great Expectations* she said was for school. I looked at young Daphne and realized that the sorrow in our assembled group had many manifestations.

Bruce and I were tasked with taking a bunch of floral arrangements to church so they would be there the next day for the Memorial service. Why they'd been sent to my mother's apartment, I had no idea. But it made as much sense as anything else, hauling them around town so we could have them with us at each stop in our grieving. I was delighted to be on an errand, any errand, just to get away from the suffocating air in the apartment, the suffocating sadness, and the bewildering narrative being pulled out of thin air by my mother, like Rumpelstiltskin spinning straw into gold.

We filled up my sister's SUV, wedged the vases in tight so they wouldn't tip over. My stomach flipped when we pulled up at the West Side Baptist Church, where I'd grown up. I'd been ostracized by the church for my rebellious behavior as a teenager, and vowed never to return. But here I was. The building was unlocked, and as we slid in a side door, we could hear women talking, banging pots and pans in the kitchen. We slunk down the dark hall with our burdens. The air in there felt sad, just like the air inside me, but otherwise not too bad.

In the foyer of the chapel, we set up the flowers beside a decorated Christmas tree. Next to the sparkly tree the flowers looked pitiful and anemic, which was fitting—any gesture made in the enormous face of death is indeed pitiful and anemic.

We tiptoed back down the hall. I heard a lady in the kitchen with a loud voice, going on and on.

"Those tongs," she said, "were from Mother's family. Sterling silver. Over 150 years old. I can't find them anywhere, and I hate to say it, but I wonder if Pearl took them."

I put out a hand to stop Bruce, and we froze outside the kitchen door.

"It's a mystery," I mouthed.

He nodded.

Another voice answered, "Heavens no, she didn't take them! She's been with us for years. I can't believe you would even suggest it. I think you put them in the Goodwill bag by mistake. You've given away things by accident before."

In the Glow of the Lavalamp

Bruce shook his finger at me as if scolding.

The loud voice said, "I think I know what I gave to Goodwill. I filled out a tax form. I'd never have given anyone Mother's tongs."

"They'll turn up," said the other voice. "Can you give me a hand with this tray?"

We eased out and closed the church door silently.

"Nancy Drew is on the case," I said.

He laughed. "Did your dad have anything like that? Maybe we could slip some into the kitchen and surprise them."

"Not really," I said. "Mom is the guardian of all things old and valuable."

***

The next day, we all dragged ourselves to church for the funeral dinner, a nice meal put on by the bereavement committee. Afterward would be the memorial service and visitation. This was more challenging, as it was not just being at church, but being with lots of church people. I wondered if they still saw me as a bad person. I wondered if I could stop seeing them as bad people. On the way over, I had a nip of wine to fortify myself and help cram my sadness into a manageable shape.

We gathered around the tables of steaming food; I could feel how those people really cared about Mom, and had loved my dad, too. Church people show love with food and they were expansive, down to three varieties of iced tea and many fresh-baked pies. I might have had a lousy history with the church, but I was warmed by the way they were taking care of Mom.

We dodged the beet Jell-O and loaded our plates with creamy and comforting chicken tetrazzini. One of the women serving food had a sonorous voice that sounded familiar. I decided she must be the one who'd lost her tongs.

I smiled and thanked the serving ladies. When they came at me with open arms, I hugged them back, turning my head to the side. Nobody said anything about the smell of alcohol. Not that they would've scolded me right there at the dinner before my dad's funeral. I was walking a thin line, trying to be considerate of everyone and their institutions, and trying to keep from sobbing, cursing, or having some kind of breakdown—whatever that might entail. I could feel myself getting close. The years in that church, most of them not good, were tugging at me, and I was dizzy with loss and confusion. I wanted to be anywhere else, thinking about anything besides my father's death. I sent Bruce out to the car to retrieve a tiny airplane-serving-size bottle of wine I had brought along just in case.

In the Glow of the Lavalamp

I put the wine in my purse and headed toward the ladies' room. The linoleum-floored hall that had seemed huge to me as kid now felt narrow and cramped. As I walked, young Daphne streaked past me, running. She was in a stall, sniffling when I came through the door. The bathroom smelled like a cave, just as it had when I was a child.

I went to the stall on the far end and chugged the wine. Liquid gold cascaded down my throat as if God himself had sent an angel, pointed, and said, "That one, she's struggling, give her some relief."

"Thank you, Jesus," I whispered, halfway meaning it. Maybe totally meaning it. It wasn't going to fix anything, but it planed the sharp edges off everything for the moment.

I wrapped the empty bottle in toilet paper and put it in the Kotex disposal bin. Then I sat and did some deep breathing and wondered where I might get more wine. After a bit, I flushed as a formality, came out and washed my hands, and so did Daphne.

I looked at her tear-streaked face in the mirror and said, "What's wrong?"

After making me promise not to tell anyone, she said, "My stepmom and I are staying at Miss Mabel and Miss Dolores's house. They're nice, but I didn't want to come at all. There's a party at my friend Caitlan's house, and I'm missing it."

"I'm sorry," I said. "It seems so unfair, when you didn't even know who died."

"I know." She scowled. "It's not fair. Did you know him?"

"Yeah," I said. "I did. We'll get to that, but tell me about staying at Miss Mabel's house."

"Well, they're nice, but they stare at me all the time." She bugged her eyes out. "And I'm not allowed to play my iPod."

"That sounds hard."

"Yeah," she said. "It's hard. It's boring, and everyone is sad. When Miss Mabel's brother came over, I broke a teacup by accident. I didn't mean to. The bad part is, I…I had to use the bathroom."

I nodded, welcoming the diversion, any diversion.

"But when I used it, I had a big, I mean it was really big…" she held her hands about twelve inches apart, and her face went dark red.

"You mean a large bowel movement?"

She nodded, her face drawn. "Yeah, that. So long it wouldn't flush. I tried a bunch of times. But it wouldn't break. And it was too big to swirl and too long to go head first. I mean if it had a head."

"Oh."

"I didn't know what to do!"

"I wouldn't know either," I said, thinking, *Welcome to the world of grownups, and faking it.*

"But I couldn't just leave it there." She stared at me, tearing up.

"So what did you do?"

"I got a bag from the kitchen, and the salad tongs."

"A plastic bag?" I asked.

"All they had was paper!"

"So you bagged it?"

"Yeah," she said. "I grabbed it with the tongs and put it in the bag."

"What did you do with the bag?"

"I threw it up in a tree in the back yard."

"In a tree?"

"Well I had to get rid of it!" She stared at me, her face pleading, and chewed on a lock of hair.

"Yeah," I said, "I get it. And the tongs?" I tried to sound only mildly curious.

"I put them in the bag before I threw it up in the tree."

"Oh." A big smile spread across my face, and I barked a little cough to keep from guffawing.

"And now Miss Mabel thinks somebody stole her tongs! I didn't think they'd notice. But I couldn't put them back in the kitchen all dirty..."

"Of course not," I said, as if the only logical thing would be to toss them up into the branches of a tree in a paper bag along with the giant turd they'd retrieved.

Tears rolled down her face. "Now somebody's going to get in trouble because I stole the tongs."

"You didn't steal them," I said, giggling. "Those tongs are still on their property. They just don't know exactly where."

"But they're mad."

I laughed until I cried. We sat there on the big flowered sofa in the ladies room, and she cried and I cried, and we both laughed. She missed her dad, recently spun off in divorce. I said I missed mine, too.

"I'm glad you're here, Daphne," I said. "You're my favorite person I've met at this funeral."

"Why?"

"Sitting here talking with you is the best I've felt in a long time."

She wrinkled her nose and looked at me like I might be crazy. "Because why?"

"Because laughing makes everything a little bit better," I said. "I'm glad you threw that bag of…stuff up in the tree."

"But what about the tongs?" she asked, twirling her hair. "I didn't know they were valuable."

"They're not gone forever. Next time it rains, that bag will come apart and fall out of the tree, and somebody will find the tongs in the back yard."

Her eyes opened wide. "What if somebody steals them? Or runs over them with the lawn mower? And what about the, the big, uh—"

"Don't worry about that. They'll think it's from a dog," I said. "A big dog. Happens all the time. And we can get the tongs back. We can go get them." I was getting an overwhelming urge to flex my adult power and set the world right, or at least this little piece of the world. "We'll get them and put them on the back porch where Miss Mabel can find them."

"How?"

"It would be my pleasure. We'll go this evening after the funeral; you can come with us, if you want. My boyfriend is good at sports and climbing, and problem solving, and he'll climb up and get them or shake them down."

***

The funeral was a blur. Papa's ninety-two-year-old brother lost track of himself while leading the prayer and segued into some stories about my father. He never said "Amen." After a while he just stopped talking and stepped away from the pulpit, looking confused.

At the visitation, I shook hands with many people, most of whom I barely knew, or didn't know at all. It was flu season, and I didn't want to shake all those hands. I could tell they wished us well, wished us comfort, and still I wanted it to be over. The Christmas tree gave me something to stare at, and my five-year-old nephew plowed into it several times. I hoped he would knock it over, giving us all a new and fixable disaster to focus on, but the thing remained upright. We were all glad when the visiting finally shut down and we could gather up the photo album, the guest register, and once again, the floral arrangements, and leave. I suggested that Daphne might want to ride back with Bruce and me.

But her step-mom had other plans to whisk her off to see some relatives. Daphne cried and clutched *Great Expectations*.

I pulled her aside and promised to go get the tongs. I knew that Bruce would find it good fun to go on a mission to retrieve a treetop bag containing a giant turd and some 150-year-old silver. For me it was a welcome alternative to a roomful of loud, sad relatives. It was the kind of adventure my dad would have been game for—he would have laughed. A lot.

We parked a block away from Miss Mabel's and silently walked up the street, still wearing our funeral clothes. The sun had set, and we slipped into the back yard and surveyed the trees in the dusk. One was an Osage, and large, bumpy mock oranges were all over the ground. We soon spotted what had to be the bag in the upper branches of an old hackberry.

"That kid has a good arm," said Bruce.

"I'm sure she's quite an athlete," I said. "And desperation is a great motivator."

He watched as I threw horse apples and sticks at the tree, my breath hanging in the cold air. I threw badly, over and over again, coming nowhere near the bag. I kept on heaving the mock oranges, and the thudding of them on the tree trunk felt good. In my world where everything had gone sideways, here was something concrete, a tree trunk being smacked by mock oranges.

After watching me throw for a while, Bruce asked if I wanted help. I nodded and put my hands in my coat pockets to warm them. He knocked the bag down on his second try. I gave a little whoop, and lights went on in Mabel and Dolores's house. We crouched behind the shrubbery. When the lights went back out, we nabbed the bag, shook the now-bent giant turd onto the frozen grass in the moonlight, and used the crunchy paper to pick up the tongs.

Back in the car, I cleaned them, using an entire roll of paper towels and the "Green Cleaner" left over from scrubbing my father's bloody vomit out of the carpet. Bruce watched, not saying a word.

With the heater cranking, the car smelled like feces and Green Cleaner and evergreens.

Cleaning the tongs felt like some kind of ritual. Like a holiday tradition, both nonsensical and meaningful. As I did it, I wished good for Daphne and my dad, the excreters of messy substances, and all others who did the same—humans, in short. I thought of the Buddhist prayer, "May you be well, may you be happy, may you be free from suffering." And I wished that for all of us. I sat there rubbing the tongs with a paper towel and thinking.

These bodies of ours carry around our joys, our longings, our losses, and expel fluids and squeeze out turds too big for standard plumbing. These houses of our souls will have their say. And when they fail or confound us, we reach out, try to keep the best face on, and clean up after each other.

In the Glow of the Lavalamp

ACKNOWLEDGEMENTS

Many people helped to make this book possible. I am fortunate indeed. I'm grateful to all the people who passed along their experiences and permitted me to tweak them for the stories in this book. The struggles and challenges are real as well as funny, and they connect us with people everywhere.

Big thanks to the Nashville Writers, where I have been encouraged along the path from the day I walked into my first meeting.

Feedback from friends and writing peers has been incredibly helpful. I thank Kathleen Cosgrove, Robert Mangeot, Brenda McClain, and Jonathan Hart Price for their ongoing patience, perseverance, and clear-headed feedback. Others who have read and commented on early drafts of stories include Annie Tench, Rob Stapleton, Nick Blanton, Gary Jenkins, Ed Pierce, Paige Tench, Eric Lewis, Marianne Tamburro, Gigi Nashville, Sherry Wilds, Lisa Baker, and the many

Acknowledgements

members of the Novelist, Humor, Mystery, and Craft of Writing groups—I say thank you to each of you for your help. Darnell Arnolt, gifted and generous writing teacher, writer, and human being, has taught me a lot and heartened me to keep going.

Professional editing from Michael Abrahamson and Jennifer Chesak has been a Godsend. I so appreciate the patience and artistic skill of Dan Chaffee in creating the cover art and cover for this book.

Special thanks to Melanie Vare, Chris Pilny, Autumn Rigsby Jones, Christy Bradley James, Kristin Chapman Gibbons, Kathleen Cosgrove, Patsy and Herman Lawson, and Michael McRay for welcoming my tales to your shows.

Many people cheered me on, and I would not be where I am without the laughter, support, and enthusiasm of Anna Chytil, Dan Chaffee, Marianne Tamburro, Kathleen Cosgrove, Ed Pierce, Janet Neely, and Rob Stapleton. Y'all have been my floaty-wings. Thank you.